Benedikte Rathmann Hansen

Sensational Slippers

30 Trendy, Cozy, Dainty, and Practical Designs for Comfy Stylish Feet

Translated by Carol L. Schroeder

TRAFALGAR SQUARE
North Pomfret, Vermont

First published in the United States of America in 2009 by
Trafalgar Square Books, North Pomfret, Vermont 05053

Originally published in the Danish language by
Forlaget Olivia, København, Denmark

ISBN: 978-1-57076-431-8
Library of Congress Control Number: 2008937235

Photographs by Kira Brandt
Illustrations by Benedikte Rathmann Hansen, Trine Andresen and
Hanne Jacobsen
Graphic design by Sisterbrandt designstue
Publishing house editor: Louise Klindt

Printed in China

10 9 8 7 6 5 4 3 2 1

Contents

Preface

· ·

I have created this book of slipper designs for the whole family. You will find winter slippers made of felt, crocheted summer slippers, and beautiful, thick knitted slippers. Hundreds of beads are used on the slippers, and just as many stories played in my head as I sewed on the beads, felted, knitted, crocheted, took out stitches and reworked them.

To me, craft work is a love story that can be told no matter what else is happening in your life. It is by working with our hands that we find peace, and it is by working with our hands that we can safely experiment with the most dramatic adventures, and find ourselves and each other in an otherwise busy world.

The patterns in this book are not intended for beginners—but begin anyway! It's not so hard. Ask a friend to help, or look in a book that has basic handcraft techniques. It is best if you can made a sample that is right for your size, so you don't have to modify the pattern while you're working on it. Get started, have fun, and make each project your own! Join in the telling of tales, and never stop.

All my best,
Benedikte Rathmann Hansen

Detail from Tulip-colored slippers, see page 70

Projects

FELTED SLIPPERS

Water Lilies, page 19

Ram's Horn, page 22

Winter's Eve, page 24

Citrus Fruits, page 25

Japanese Tabi Socks with Sequins, page 26

Japanese Tabi Socks for Men, page 28

Whales, page 30

French Slippers, page 33

Wasp Stings, page 34

Bark, page 37

KNITTED AND FELTED SLIPPERS

Warm Leggings, page 39

Hyacinth, page 40

Flower, page 42

Tulips, page 45

Aqua, page 46

KNITTED SLIPPERS

Springtime, page 49

Greek, page 52

Heartwarmers, page 54

Soft Skies, page 56

My Shoes, page 57

CROCHETED SLIPPERS

Strawberry-colored Summer Slippers, page 60

Mouse, page 62

Hedgehog, page 65

Summer Slippers, page 68

Tulip-colored Slippers, page 70

Knobby Boots, page 75

Beads, page 79

Sunshine Boots, page 82

Winter-blue Slippers with Ice Crystals, page 85

Happy Stripes, page 87

Before you begin

Abbreviations
ch = chain stitch (crochet)
CO = cast on (knitting)
dec = decrease
fs = first stitch
hdc = half double crochet
   (in UK, half treble stitch)
inc = increase
k = knit
k2tog = knit 2 together
lp st = loop stitch (crochet)
ls = last stitch
p = purl
psso = pass the slipped stitch over
rnd = round
rep = repeat
sc = single crochet (in UK, double
crochet)
sl st = slip stitch (in UK,
   single crochet)
st = stitch, stitches
w & t = wrap and turn
yo = yarn over (knitting)
yo = yarn over (crochet)

Felting
This section is intended as an introduction to the felting process, but you can also use it as a reference if there is something you're uncertain of.

Wool
I have chosen to use wool roving such as Merino and Corriedale for the felted slippers. You could even combine these two types of wool, if you like. They work well together.

Merino is not the most durable wool, but I've had good experience in using it for slippers. It is very soft, and not scratchy. It can be found in a variety of colors that would inspire anyone.

Corriedale is also available in many delightful colors, and is very easy to work with. It has a nice shine to it and is well suited to slippers.

Resists
A resist, or template, is a form that you use to felt around. You can use corrogated cardboard, fabric lining material, a foam rubber pad or any similar material to make the resist. Try to find a material that is thick enough so you can feel its edges through the wool as you are working. In this way you will avoid ugly creases.

Template A
This style of resist is based on two patterns – one for each foot. Draw around the outline of your foot on a piece of paper, and remember to hold the pencil upright as you draw.

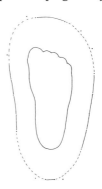

Template A

Enlarge the foot patterns with the help of the table below. Draw a smooth curve along the length and width, as shown. Cut out two identical resists using the material of your choice.

Add to the foot's width	Add to the foot's length
Child 1.25"(3 cm)	1.75" (4.5 cm)
Woman 1.5" (4 cm)	2.5" (6 cm)
Man 1.75" (4.5 cm)	2.75" (7 cm)

Template B

With this pattern, both of the slippers are felted simultaneously. When it is time to remove the resist, you simply cut the work down the center, so that you have two separate slippers to continue felting.

Draw around your foot with an upright pencil. Imagine that the inner side of your foot is the bottom of the sole of a boot, and create a smooth profile using the curve of your toes and your heel. Draw a little ankle section coming up from the boot. Now fold the paper (the dotted line in the illustration) and mirror the outline of your boot. Enlarge the template using the table above, and cut the resist out of your material of choice.

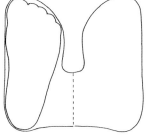

Template B

Dividing the wool

Before the wool roving can be laid out, it needs to be divided into equal piles. You don't need to use a scale for this. Both types of wool are sold in hanks that you can just pull lightly on in order to divide them.

Laying out the wool

Lay the wool out in a crossways pattern, as shown in the drawings on this page and the one that follows. When you lay the wool sideways on your resist, allow it to extend 1.25" to 1.5" (3 to 4 cm) beyond the edges of the pattern, but not out over the toe or heel. When you lay it lengthwise over the resist, allow it to extend 1.25" to 1.5" (3 to 4 cm) beyond the heel and toes, but not over the sides.

Lay the wool sideways across on the resist

When the directions state that the wool should be laid out in two cross-layers, it means that you should create one layer sideways across the resist and one lengthwise. Four cross-layers means that you should begin with a sideways layer, then add one lengthwise, one sideways and then a final layer lengthwise.

Make sure the wool is even so that the layers are equally thick overall. It will take quite a bit of wool for each layer.

Lay the wool lengthwise across on the resist

The Resist is Packed with Wool

Use a roasting pan in order to avoid having the water splash you. Lay a piece of gardisette, (see page 15) in the bottom of the roasting pan. This fabric should be larger than your layers of wool. Now put the layers of wool, which will be along one side of the resist into the roasting pan. Carefully wet the wool, keeping the edges dry. Lay the resist on top of the wool layers and fold the edges over the wool in over the resist. You might want to dampen the resist a bit so that the edges lay down flatter. Then add the layers of wool on top of the resist for the other side. Put another layer of gardisette on top, and wet the wool. Be sure to go all the way out to the edges. Take hold of the entire project, including the bottom layer of gardisette, and turn it over. Remove the gardisette and fold the last edges in to wrap around the resist. Remember to be certain that the wool is now wet. Lay the piece of gardisette on top again, and begin to hand felt very carefully.

Felting Technique

There are many ways to felt—and new ones are always being invented. I am going to explain how I felted the slippers in this book, but remember that other felting techniques can certainly be used.

1. If you are felting a design that will use lining felt to hold it together, step number 2 may need more time.

About 15 minutes of hand felting with the gardisette still over the work, being especially careful to work the wool all the way out to the edges of the resist. Use small, rotating movements.

2. 15-30 minutes using an electric vibrating sander with plastic on it instead of sandpaper, or rolling in a rubber or bamboo mat, or sheet of bubble wrap with small bubbles. At some point in this process the resists will bulge out. Cut them out, and hand felt the slippers on the inside and out. Check to make sure that the edges are smooth and don't have ugly ridges. Continue using the sander or rolling the slippers, taking care to continually fold them in different ways so that you don't get any unattractive creases. Turn the slippers inside-out and continue to felt, then turn them right-side out again.

3. If the work is firm and the edg-

es don't show an inclination to felt together, it is now time to felt the slippers in the washing machine. Set the water temperature at 86 degrees F (30 degrees C). It is not necessary to use soap, as there is already soap in the slippers. Let the machine wash the slippers, checking regularly so that you can take them out before they have shrunk too much or gotten too far out of shape.

4. Put the slipper on and felt it in warm soapy water until it is the right size for your foot. Finish the process as described in the section entitled Rinsing and Steaming below.

Rinsing

When the slippers are completely finished being felted, rinse them thoroughly and lay them in a solution of water and vinegar for 15 minutes to neutralize any detergent remaining. Use about ¼ cup (1/2 deciliter) of vinegar for 1 quart (1 liter) of water. The slippers can now be put in the spin cycle of a washing machine, formed again and dried.

Steaming

If you steam the slippers, they will hold their shape longer. Take a large pot, fill the bottom with water, and put the slippers in the pot on a vegetable steaming rack. The slippers must not touch the water. Put the lid on the pot (it should not fit too tightly), and steam the slippers for one hour. Make sure that the pot doesn't boil dry. Take the slippers out carefully and lay them out to dry.

Lining Felt

Lining felt is a type of thin "wool paper" which you can cut shapes out of, and which you can if you wish felt onto your slippers. Lay the wool out in two or four layers of cross-patterns, and felt until the work has shrunk about 20%. Cut out the shape you desire, lay it on to the slippers, and felt it onto them with gardisette on top. Hand felt the slippers using warm, soapy water and a firm touch, or use the electric finishing sander with the plastic covering.

Gardisette

Gardisette, or a similar nylon mesh curtain fabric, is used to lay over your project at the beginning of the felting process, or when you want to attach a felt lining, for example in "Winter's Eve" and "Wasp Stings."

Lay the gardisette over the work, and rub on the gardisette instead of directly on the wool. Lift the gardisette up carefully from time to time to make sure that it doesn't get felted onto your work.

Soap

I use an unscented, vegetable-based liquid brown soap when I felt. It works well and is gentle on your skin. You can buy this soap in most yarn stores. To determine the amount to use, add the soap to warm water until the water glides smoothly between your fingers.

You can also use dishwashing soap, fill washing machine with hot water at lowest water level and add 1-2 tablespoons.

Knitting

The knitted designs in this book are mostly soft and plush, and easy to make.

Yarn Choices

I have chosen soft, smooth yarns for most of the knitted designs—and not necessarily the most durable types of yarn. If you want to extend the life of your slippers, you can add soles to them or knit them in a more durable yarn. Remember to maintain the same ratio of stitches per inch if you change yarn types. Be particularly careful if you change the type of yarn for one the designs that are to be felted. Be certain that the yarn will take to the felting process. Not all yarns can be felted, even if they are wool.

Increasing

When the instructions state "increase 1" or "take a one stitch increase," it means that you should add one stitch at the beginning and one at the end of the row.

Seed Stitch (or Moss Stitch)

Row 1: *Knit (k) 1, purl (p) 1*, rep (repeat) from * to *.

Row 2: Purl (p) above knit, Knit (k) above purl.

Repeat the 2nd row pattern for the remainder of the work.

Casting on

When you cast on using loop casting, you create small loops (half stitches) with your fingers and then put the loops onto the knitting needle as stitches.

Fulling, or Knitted Felting

The knitted designs that are to be felted should be washed in 86 degrees F (30 degrees C) water in a washing machine along with a small amount of liquid vegetable-based brown soap or dishwashing soap. Use a blob slightly larger than a quarter. Remember to stop the washing machine periodically to check on whether the slippers are finished.

You can also hand-felt the slippers. Put warm water and soap in a bowl. The amount of soap should be enough to make the water glide through your fingers. Submerge the slippers, rub and knead them until they are the desired size.

When the slippers are finished, they should be rinsed, put in a vinegar and water solution and spun dry, as described on page 15.

Right and left slippers

Unless otherwise specified, the right and left slippers are identical.

Crocheting

Yarn Choices

You can use cotton, wool and blended yarns for the crocheted styles. Note, however, that these designs are crocheted using heavy yarn and a big crochet hook. This means that you cannot apply what the label on the yarn says about the gauge. You may need to use more strands, or fewer, to achieve the same gauge as in the patterns. You can, of course, just use the same yarn that I have used.

Creating a Chain

Chain the specified number of chs indicated in each pattern, Remember to always start in the 2nd ch from hook.

Decreasing (dec)

When you decrease, you subtract a stitch by crocheting two stitches together to make one stitch. Put the crochet hook through the first stitch, work the stitch, and then pull the crochet hook with the worked stitch through the next one. Do the same with the following stitch, which will give you three stitches on the crochet hook. Work the stitch, pulling the yarn through all three loops on the hook.

Increasing (inc)

Increase by adding a stitch. Crochet 2 stitches in the loop of the same single stitch.

First and Last Stitch

When crocheting, there are two stitches you should take particular care with: your first stitch (fs) and your last stitch (ls). In the pattern instructions I show you how to mark the first stitch in a row with a red thread and the last stitch with a blue thread. Remember to move these marker threads each time you start a new row so that you will always know where you are.

The first stitch (fs) and last stitch (ls) are marked with a thread

All of the increases in the patterns are evenly distributed on either side of the first and last stitch.

If, for example, I write: "Heel, 4 single crochet (sc) stitches, 1 decrease (dec). Toe: 1 dec, 5 sc, 1 dec. Heel 1 dec, 4 sc, 1 sc in the last stitch" this means that you start the row by decreasing one single stitch in the fifth from the last stitch in the row, and that you decrease one single crochet stitch out of the five centermost stitches at the front of the foot, and that after this you finish each row by decreasing a single stitch out at the fifth from the last stitch in the row.

Tip
Whenever possible try to weave in the yarn ends as you crochet. This will look neat and firm, and will save you a great deal of effort finishing off the ends.

Drop Yarn
When the instructions say "Drop yarn until the 9th round," it means that you should crochet half a round—in other words a round that is only crocheted on the front part of the foot. You should just drop the yarn, crochet the other half round with the second ball of yarn and then use the loop to begin when you are to crochet a full round again, and at the same time you will crochet in the ends of the half round in order to attach it.

Loop Stitch with Beads
Use a thick pencil, or whatever I recommend in the instructions. Crochet 1 to 5 single crochet stitches, depending on the design. Put the crochet hook in the next stitch, as if ready to work a single stitch. Twist the yarn around the pencil, holding it in your right hand, while you attach a single bead. The yarn should be twisted clockwise. Crochet a single stitch. Now you have a loop with a bead on it on the pencil. Continue in this manner, periodically pulling the pencil out so that it doesn't restrict your work too much.

If the directions call for "1 single stitch, loop stitches (lp st), 2 chain stitch (ch) in the sole, turn," it means that you should crochet a single stitch before you make the first loop (lp). After that you continue with loop stitches, putting the designated number of single stitches between the loops.

Right and left slippers
Unless otherwise specified, the right and left slipper are identical.

Felted slippers

It's a good idea to read the information about felting on page 12 before you start one of the felted slipper projects. You'd find lots of good tips and helpful advice.

Water Lilies

Materials: Corriedale wool in the following colors: 4.5 oz. (130 g) kiwi fruit, .75 oz. (20 g) lime, 1 oz. (30 g) candy floss as well as a little bit of yellow wool, green DMC embroidery floss, yellow and pink sewing thread, liquid latex, 9 oz. (3.5 mm) sole leather, lime colored leather dye and colorless edge finish.
Size: Women's.

For this style of slipper, you will lay the wool out on a resist. When you have finished the first slipper, lift the wool carefully off of the resist so that it can be used for the next slipper.

Make a tracing of the template on this page and enlarge or reduce it using a copier until it is the right size for your foot. Then make a second template 150% bigger. It doesn't matter if this template won't fit on a single piece of paper. Make two resists and put them both aside.

Weigh the green kiwi wool so that you have 2 piles weighing 1.5 oz. (45 grams) each for the soles, and 4 piles of .5 oz. (10 grams) each for the water lily leaves. Then divide each pile into 4 sections so that you can lay out 4 crosswise layers for the leaves and the soles, as shown on page 13.

Even though the layers will not

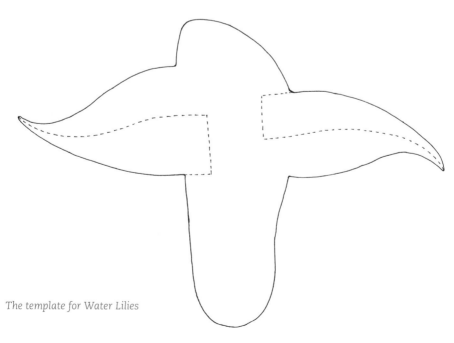

The template for Water Lilies

be the same thickness, spread the wool out as a single unit so that the leaves and the soles fit together.

It doesn't matter at all if the wool extends a bit over the resist as you make these layers.

Lay the lime colored wool out in two layers, creating a 10" X 14" (25 x 35 cm) rectangle. Do the same with the light pink wool.

Felt the entire piece together thoroughly. You should also make two small felted balls about ½" (1 cm) in diameter with the yellow wool. Rinse the felt.

Cut the kiwi green felt following the smaller template, the one that is the right size for your foot. Cut out 4 light green leaves and 36 pink petals following the pattern. Note that the light green leaves should be lengthened by ¾" (2 cm) so that they will reach under the soles.

Sew the light green leaves on using small running stitches using green embroidery floss. When you get to the part of the leaves that curves under the soles, make sure that the stitches don't go all the way through the kiwi green felt, as this may make the slippers uncomfortable. Sew along the water lily leaves' kiwi green edges to reinforce the edges of the slipper.

The Water Lily
First lay out 6 petals, sew them on using pink thread, then continue to the next layer. Try to alternate the petals from one layer to the next so that they can all be seen. Make a total of three layers.

The Petals
Try on the slipper. Wrap the water lily leaves around your foot and pin them. Put the water lily flower in place. Stitch the leaves and flower together using yellow thread. Attach the small yellow balls at the same time as you stitch up and down through the flower and leaves. Sew carefully. The stitches you make now will be holding the whole slipper together. Tie off well.

Place the slippers onto the leather, and trace an outline of the shape of the soles. Cut them out using a sharp hobby knife. Color the edges with leather dye and then add a protective layers of colorless edge dye. Add soles on using liquid latex as described on page 91.

Pattern for the petals

Water Lilies

Ram's Horn

Materials: 6.5 oz. (180 g) cobalt blue
Merino, liquid latex.
Size: Women's.

Make two women's resists using
Template A, as shown on page 12.
Add a 6.75" (17 cm) long point at
the front of the template. Remember to round the edges a bit so that
the template doesn't work itself out
through the wool (see drawing).

Divide the wool into 16 equal piles
(8 for each slipper), and lay out four
crossways layers on each side of the
two resists, as shown on page 13. Be
careful not to put too much wool in
the pointed front of the resist.

Felt until the resist bulges out. Cut
a slit from the heel and about 3.25"
(8 cm) further up. Take the resist
out, and continue to felt the slippers
completely both inside and out.

Begin to form the points. Remember to pull them carefully into shape
so that they don't get too many
wrinkles on the top. Roll the points
often between your hands so that
they become stiff and can hold their
shape.

Rinse the slippers carefully, and
cut out the ankle holes so that they
fit. Note that this design fits high up
on the foot.

Dry the slippers with the points
in the desired shape. If you want you
can support the points by twisting
them around something (for example the handle of a wooden spoon,
a thick knitting needle, etc.) while
they dry. Steam the slippers as described on page 15.
When the slippers are once again
completely dry, add soles using liquid latex, as shown on page 90.

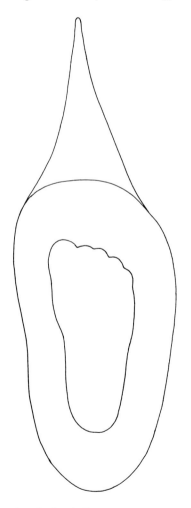

Template for Ram's Horn

Ram's Horn

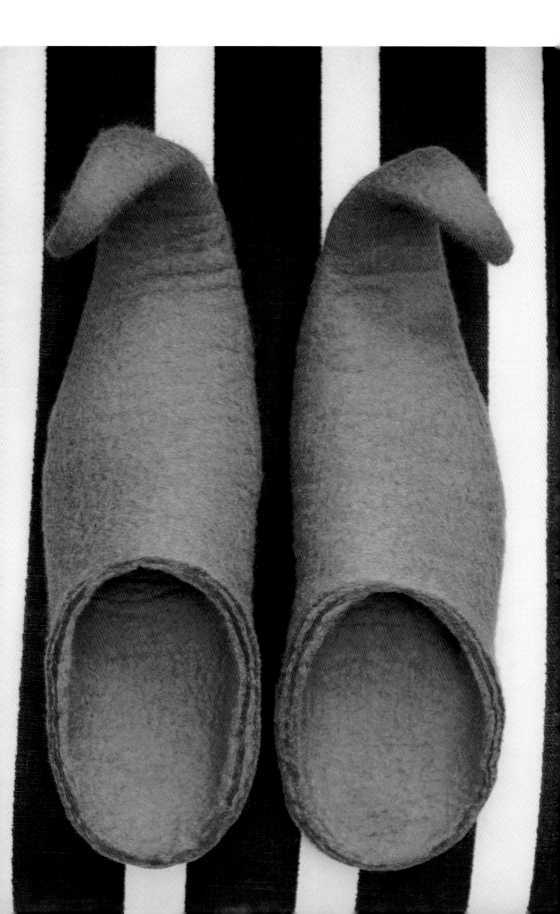

Winter's Eve

Materials: 3.5 oz. (100 g) cobalt blue Merino, approx. ¼ oz. (5 g) sun yellow Merino, white and yellow DMC embroidery floss, liquid latex.
Size: Child's.

Make two children's resists based on Template A on page 12.

Lay the yellow wool out in four cross-way layers measuring about 3.5" X 7" (9 X 18 cm) create the lining felt as shown on page 15. Cut out two round moons and put them aside.

Divide the blue wool into 16 piles (8 for each slipper), and lay out four crossways layers on each side of the resists. Felt until the resists bulge out. Cut a slit along the round end of the heel and remove the resists. Felt the yellow moons onto the inside of the heels. If this is difficult, you can attach them with a felting needle or a few stitches using yellow thread.

Continue felting the slippers thoroughly both inside and out. Cut the opening into shape. Rinse, dry and steam the slippers as described on page 15.

Embroider the snowflakes using French knots and stars as shown on page 89. Add soles using liquid latex, as shown on page 90.

Winter's Eve

Citrus Fruits

Materials: 4.25 oz. (120 g) orange Merino, 1.75 oz. (50 g) sun yellow Merino, 2 oz. (60 g) white Merino, liquid latex.
Size: Women's.

Make two women's resists using Template A as shown on page 12.

Divide the orange wool into 16 equal piles (8 for each slipper), and lay four layers of crossways pattern as described on page 13. Divide the yellow wool into 8 piles, and make two layers on each side of the resist. In the same manner, divide the white wool into 8 piles and make two crossways layers of it on each side of the resists. Felt until the resists bulge out. Cut a slit about 3.25" (8 cm) in on the heel. Take the resists out, and continue to felt the slippers thoroughly both inside and out. Draw the hole for the foot using a piece of chalk. Note that this design has a little rise at the back of the heel. Cut out the hole. Keep the part you've trimmed away so that you have a piece of felt to practice cutting holes in.

Rinse, dry and steam the slippers.

With a pair of sharp scissors, cut ½"-¾" (1-2 cm.) slits in the slippers' uppers and in the heel cap by folding the felt and holding it tightly in one hand while you cut with the other. It is important that you not cut into the orange wool, but take out enough white and yellow wool so that the orange wool will show through. Turn the work periodically so that some of the slits face in one direction and others in another.

Add soles using liquid latex, as shown on page 90.

Citrus Fruits

Japanese Tabi Socks with Sequins

Materials: 4.5 oz. (130 g) Corriedale scarlet, 200 light blue sequins, light blue sewing thread, liquid latex. Size: Women's.

Create two resists with a separate section for the big toe. Draw an outline of your foot on a piece of paper, remembering to include a space between the big toe and the other toes. Then cut a straight slit in by the big toe and spread it outwards. Add about ¾" (2 cm) to the width of the big toe on both sides and 1.5" (4 cm) to the big toe's length, as well as 1.25" (3 cm) to the width of the other toes and 2.5" (6 cm) to their length; 1.5" (4 cm) to the width of the foot on both sides and 2.5" (6 cm) to the heel. Draw around the outline.

Divide the wool into 16 piles (8 for each slipper) and lay out 4 crossways layers on each side of each resist.

Felt until the resists bulge out. Cut a slit along the curve of the heel and remove the resists. Continue to felt the slippers thoroughly on the inside and out. Be especially careful felting the pieces that will come between the big toe and the other toes. Cut the opening into shape. Try the slippers on, and felt long and well.

Rinse, dry and steam the slippers, as shown on page 15. Sew on the sequins, and add the soles using liquid latex, as shown on page 90.

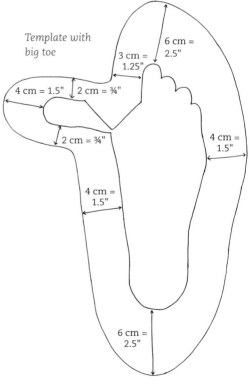

Template with big toe

6 cm = 2.5"

3 cm = 1.25"

4 cm = 1.5" 2 cm = ¾"

2 cm = ¾"

4 cm = 1.5"

4 cm = 1.5"

6 cm = 2.5"

Draw around your foot

Japanese Tabi Socks with Sequins

Japanese Tabi Socks for Men

Materials: 5.25 oz. (150 g) Merino wool, liquid latex.
Size: Men's.

Create two resists with a separate section for the big toe. Draw an outline of your foot on a piece of paper, remembering to include a space between the big toe and the other toes. as shown on page 26. Then cut a straight slit in by the big toe and spread it outwards. Add about 1" (2.5 cm) to the width of the big toe on both sides and 1.75" (4.5 cm) to the big toe's length, as well as 1.5" (3.5 cm) to the width of the other toes and 2.75" (7 cm) to their length; 1.75" (4.5 cm) to the width of the foot on both sides and 2.75" (7 cm) to the heel. Draw around this outline.

Divide the wool into 16 piles (8 for each slipper) and lay out 4 crossways layers on each side of each resist.

Felt until the resists bulge out. Cut a slit along the curve of the heel and remove the resists. Continue to felt the slippers thoroughly on the inside and out. Be especially careful felting the pieces that will come between the big toe and the other toes. Cut the opening into shape. Try the slippers on, and felt long and well.

Rinse, dry and steam the slippers, as shown on page 15. Add the soles using liquid latex, as shown on page 90.

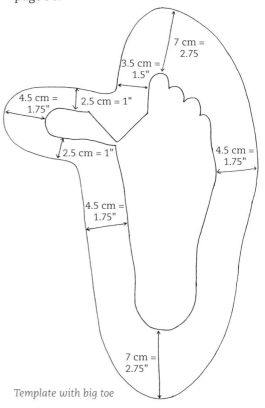

Template with big toe

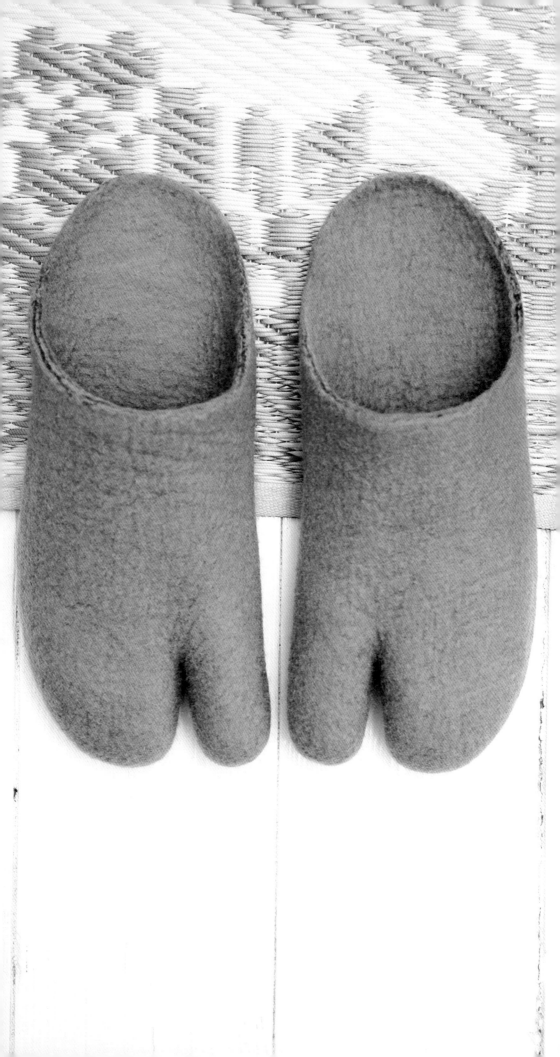

Whales

Materials: 3.5 oz. (100 g) Corriedale color bean sprout, a bit of black and white wool, red, black and white DMC embroidery floss, liquid latex.
Tools: 1 cotton cloth, 2 empty toilet paper tubes, 2 pins, about 1 yd. (1 m) ribbon or bias tape.
Size: Child's.

Make a resist for a pair of children's slippers using Template B on page 13. Remember to lengthen the shank (cuff) between the two feet in the pattern, as you will actually be felting low boots rather than slippers.

Divide the wool into 8 even piles, and lay out four layers in a crossways pattern on each side of the resist, as shown on page 13.

The remnants of black and white wool are for making the whale's eyes. Lay them out in four crossways patterns and felt them at the same time that you felt the boots.

Pattern for the eyes

Felt until the resists bulge out. Cut the work down the center so that you have two little boots. Remove the re-sists and continue to felt the boots thoroughly on the inside and out. Rinse them and allow them to dry.

Draw the tails of the whales on using chalk according to the pattern below, and cut them out with a sharp pair of scissors. Cut out the rest of the boot's opening, trying to get the top of the boot to come as far up on the foot as possible.

Turn on your iron, using the cotton setting. Laying a wet cotton cloth over the tails and press them flat. Repeat this several times, and as you do so bend the tails backwards so that they fit around the upright toilet paper tubes. Bend the tails around the toilet paper tubes and fasten them in place with a piece of ribbon held by a pin. Let the whales dry, and then steam them with the toilet paper tubes in place, as explained on page 15.

Cut out the 4 pieces for the eyes using the patterns on this page, and sew them on using a button-hole stitch. Use white embroidery floss for the white part and black for the black section. Stitch a long, red mouth using chain stitch embroidery.

Add soles using liquid latex, as shown on page 90.

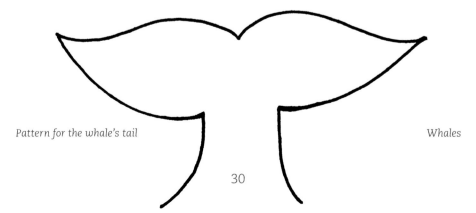

Pattern for the whale's tail

Whales

French Slippers

Materials: 4.5 oz. (130 g) Merino wool, 20" X 20" (50 x 50 cm) agave-colored silk chiffon, 20" X 20" (50 x 50 cm) turquoise silk chiffon, about 200 assorted glass beads in shades of green and turquoise, green or turquoise sewing thread, liquid latex, 9 oz. (3.5 mm) sole leather, lime colored leather dye, colorless edge finish.
Size: Women's.

Make two women's resists using Template A on page 12. Cut out two pieces of silk chiffon in each color. These pieces should extend about 2.75" (7 cm) beyond the edge of the template in the front half of the foot and follow the edges of the template on the back half of the foot, as shown in the drawing on this page.

Divide the wool into 16 even piles (8 for each slipper), and lay four layers in a crossways pattern onto each side of the resists. Wet the wool and felt lightly—only for about 5 minutes. Lay the agave-colored silk chiffon on top, and then the turquoise. Sew the chiffon onto the wool using the sewing thread. Use large stitches, attaching the glass beads as you sew. Then hand-felt, using gardisette, for about 15 minutes.

Felt until the resists bulge out. Cut a slit at the round end of the heel and remove the resists. Continue to felt the slippers thoroughly on the inside

French Slippers

and out. Shape the slippers so that they are slightly pointed in the front.

Cut the edge of the top of the slipper into shape as a long, wide tongue and finish felting, at the same time forming the top of the slipper so that it bends into a nice arch. Also trim the sole of the slipper to create a little arch in the space between the top of the slipper and the sole. This will look cute when the slipper is viewed in profile.

Rinse the slippers thoroughly, shape them, and let them dry. Trace around the slippers with chalk so you know what shape the soles should be. Cut the soles out of the leather, dye the edges and finish them with the clear edge finish. Glue the soles on as described on page 91.

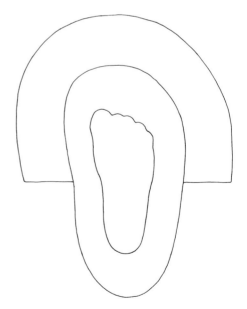

Cut the pieces of chiffon so that they are 2.75" (7 cm) wider than the edge of the template at the front of the foot, and follow the pattern at the back of the foot.

Wasp Stings

Materials: 5.25 oz. (150 g) ice blue merino, 3/4 oz. (20 g) orange merino, strong sewing thread, liquid latex.
Size: Men's.

Make two men's resists using Template A on page 12. Add a 4" (10 cm) point at the top of the templates. Remember to round the points slightly, as shown on page 22, so that the resists don't poke out through the wool.

Lay the orange wool in four layers of crossways pattern about 14" X 16" (35 X 40 cm), and follow the instructions for creating pieces of lining felt described on page 15. Cut out a total of 12 orange stripes using the patterns on this page.

Divide the ice blue wool into 16 even piles (8 for each slipper), and lay four layers of crossways pattern on each side of the resists. Be careful not to get too much wool in the points of the resists. Wet the wool, and felt it lightly (only for about 5 minutes). Divide the stripes evenly and felt them into the rest of the work by covering them with gardisette, as on page 15.

Felt until the resists bulge out. Cut a slit at the round end of the heel and remove the resists. Continue to felt the slippers thoroughly on the inside and out.

About halfway through the felting process cut the opening for the foot in its final form. Then take a piece of strong sewing thread and tuck under the edges of the orange stripes, sewing them on using a basting cross-stitch. Allow about 8" (20 cm) of thread to hang loose at each end of the stripes so that you can easily pull them out later.

Finish felting the slippers, and shape them so that the point in the front extends nicely.

Rinse, dry and steam the slippers, as described on page 15. Remove the stitches and use liquid latex to add the soles, as shown on page 90.

Pattern for the stripes. Cut out a total of 12 stripes: 2 little ones, 2 of the next size, 2 medium and 6 large. Use 6 for each slipper.

Wasp Stings

Bark

Materials: 5.25 oz. (150 g) Corriedale color licorice, 3.5 oz. (100 g) Corriedale color nutmeg, 20" X 22" (50 x 55 cm) dark brown 4 to 5 oz. leather (1.5-2 mm thick), buckles FB 187-38, liquid latex.
Size: Men's.

Make two men's resists using Template A on page 12.

Divide the black wool into 16 even piles (8 for each slipper), and lay four layers of crossways pattern on each side of the resists, as shown on page 13. Felt lightly. Divide the brown wool into 8 even piles, and lay two layers of crossways patterns on each side of the resists.

Felt until the resists bulge out. Cut a slit at the round end of the heel and remove the resists. Continue to felt the slippers thoroughly on the inside and out.

Cut the final hole for the opening for the foot about halfway through the felting process. Felt thoroughly, then rinse, dry and steam the slippers as shown on page 15.

Use a sharp hobby knife to cut 1.25" to 1.5" (3 to 4 cm) parallel slits in the upper section of the slippers to create the surface design. The knife should cut through the brown wool and down to the black, but not into the black wool. Cut a little more brown wool away from each slit using a sharp pair of scissors so that the black wool is visible through each slit.

Soles and Straps

Place one of the slippers on a large piece of tracing paper and outline it with a pencil held upright. Draw a dotted line through the middle of the sole, as shown in figure 1 on the next page.

Fold the slipper in half lengthwise, and lay it out flat on the sole you have just drawn. The fold of the sole should lie along the dotted line you drew before. Now you can draw the shape for the slipper's opening. Draw also slightly further down on the top of the slipper. This will be the center line for the strap. Then fold the slipper to the other side and repeat the process, as shown in figure 2.

Draw an outline of the straps 1.5" (38 mm) wide. Make one end of the strap 1.5" (4 cm) longer, and cut out the sole and strap shapes as shown in figure 3. Tape a piece of tracing paper on the end of the strap that you haven't made longer, as shown in figure 4. You will use this when it comes time to draw the pointed edge of the strap.

Try the slipper onto the form to see if it fits. Make any necessary adjustments. At the same time draw the point of the strap, which should be 2.75" to 3.5" (8-9 cm) long, based on your preference.

Cut the soles out of the dark

Bark

brown leather. Rough up the leather and apply liquid latex both on the soles and the straps. Give the slippers 2 to 3 layers of liquid latex, including where you want the strap to be placed.

Iron the soles in place once they have dried.

Try the slippers on again to see where the buckle should be located. Make a 1.25" (3 mm) hole with a hole punch in the short end of strap for the prong. Fold the leather down, and glue it together with liquid latex. Now attach the buckle. Give the strap time to attach itself to the top of the slipper. Make a 1.25" (3 mm) hole in the longer side of the strap in the same manner, glue it to the top of the slipper, and buckle the strap together.

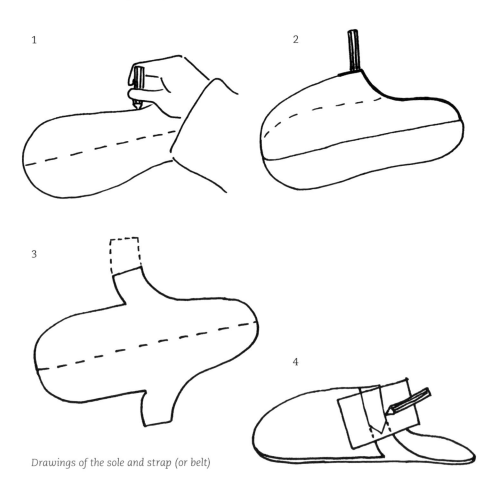

1

2

3

4

Drawings of the sole and strap (or belt)

Felted and Knitted Slippers

Warm Leggings

Materials: 7 oz. (200 g) white merino, 4 skeins Løve Baby and Hose Yarn color # 30, 1 skein Fonty Kidopale # 296, 1 skein Roma Løvegarn # 11.
Needle: Size 3, 16" circular needle
Size: Women's.

Make a woman's resist using Template B on page 13.

Divide the wool into 8 even piles, and lay four layers of crossways pattern on each side of the resist, as shown on page 13. Felt until the resist bulges out. Cut the work in the middle and remove the resist. Continue to felt the slippers thoroughly on the inside and out.

Rinse, dry and steam the slippers as shown on page 15. Add soles using liquid latex, as shown on page 90.

Variations on Warm Leggings called Speedy Stripes and Soft Romantic

Legwarmers

With size 3, 16" circular needle and 2 strands of yarn (1 of Fonty and 1 of Roma) loosely CO 132. Knit 7 rounds of rib (k2, p2). Switch to the Hose Yarn, and continue to knit rib until the work measures 24" (60 cm). Bind off loosely, and sew the legwarmers onto the slippers. Sew about ½" (1 cm) up into the first row of stitches on the legwarmers, taking care that the sewing can't be seen on the right side of the work.

Pattern for the flower for the Soft Romantic leggings

Hyacinth

Materials: 3.5 oz. (100 g) Merino hyacinth, 2 skeins Løve Baby and Hose Yarn color # 71, about 62 clear 3 mm glass beads, 22 translucent yellow 1.5 mm glass beads, 308 clear 1.5 mm glass beads, 132 mother-of-pearl white 1.5 mm glass beads, hyacinth colored sewing thread, and white sewing thread or beading cord.
Needles: Size 1 (U.K. size 2½) double point needles, also a beading needle
Size: Child's.

Make one child's resist using Template B on page 13.

Divide the wool into 8 even piles, and lay four layers of crossways pattern on each side of the resist, as shown on page 13. Felt until the resist bulges out. Cut the work in the middle and remove the resist. Continue to felt the slippers thoroughly on the inside and out. Rinse, dry and steam the slippers as shown on page 15. Add soles using liquid latex, as shown on page 90.

40

Decoration

Cut a teardrop-shaped hole in the slippers' uppers using the pattern on this page. Sew the large, clear beads along the edge of the hole using the hyacinth-colored thread. Use slipstitch, adding one bead on each stitch.

Legwarmers

With size 1 double point needles loosely CO 100. Knit rib (k2, p2) until the work measures 10" (25 cm). Bind off loosely, and sew the legwarmers onto the slippers in the same way as shown for Warm Leggings on page 40.

Beaded Edging

Note that there is no beading above the 12 center stitches at the top of the foot.

Start by attaching the thread be-tween the 6th and 7th st from the center stitch

Row 1: Put 7 clear, 1 white, 1 yellow and then 2 more white beads onto the thread. Insert the needle again through the yellow beads.

Row 2: Put 2 white beads onto the thread. Insert the needle again through the yellow beads.

Row 3: Put 1 white and 7 clear beads onto the thread. Skip 8 st, and then stitch the end of this arch onto the legwarmer.

Repeat these three rows a total of 11 times. Tie off securely.

Pattern for the teardrop-shaped opening on Hyacinth

Hyacinth

Flower

Materials: 2 skeins Fonty Angora # 336, a little bit of white merino, yellow DMC embroidery floss.
Needles: Size 4 (U.K. size 3½)
Gauge: 26 st x 54 rows in garter stitch on size 4 needles = 4" X 4" (10 x 10 cm).
Size: Girl's shoe size 8 1/2-12 (European sizes 26-30), depending on how long the slippers are felted.

Start with the cuff: * With size 4 (3 ½ UK) needle CO 34 and k 4.5" (11 cm) in stockinette stitch.*. Break the yarn, repeat from * to *, then put both pieces onto the same needle. Put the first 6 st from the first piece and the last 6 st from the second piece onto waste yarn. There are now 56 st left on the needle.

Begin foot shaping: Continue to K 2.75" (7 cm) in stockinette stitch. Decrease the first st on either side of every other row a total of 7 times, and after that decrease one st on each side of every row a total of 6 times so that here are 30 st on the needle.

Toe/stem detail: Divide the work onto two needles with 15 st on each, and knit each half separately the rest of the way. *Cast on 6 st in the middle of the work for the stem using the long tail cast on method. Bind off 3 st on the outer edge in every other row, until there are 6 st left—10 rows.* Bind off. Repeat * to * in the other section.

Knit the second slipper the same way.

Assembly

Sew the slippers together inside out using the mattress stitch, as shown on page 89. Secure the ends.

Turn inside out, and felt the slippers in a washing machine with the water temperature set at , 86 degrees F (30 degrees C) until they are the correct size, making sure to shape the body and toe detail as described on page 16.

The Flower

Take the bit of white wool and lay it out in two very thin crossways layers as shown on page 13. Felt the piece until it is finished, and then cut out two little flowers using the pattern on this page. Sew the flowers onto the stems using two yellow cross-stitches that cross over each other as shown in the drawing.

Pattern for the felt flower

Sew the felt flowers on using two cross stitches that cross over each other

Flower

Tulips

Materials: 1 skein Løve Baby and Hose Yarn color # 71, about ¼ oz. (5 g) red wool, about ¼ oz. (5 g) green wool.

Needles: Size 2 (U.K. size 2½) double point needles

Size: This pattern is designed for infant sizes 6-12 months. But since it doesn't have a heel, it can be used by a wide range of sizes. As the baby grows, more and more of the leg is used to cover the foot.

You can alter the width of this design by changing the number of stitches you cast on as you start, and the slippers can be knit to any length you wish.

Circular Knitting

Knit k2, p2 the entire time, but advance the pattern by 1 st each time you have completed 2 rounds. If you for ex. begin with k2, knit p1, k2, p2, etc. You can put a marking thread at the beginning of the round so that you will remember to advance the pattern.

On size 2 double point needles loosely CO 44, and knit in the round until the work measures 7.25" (18.5 cm) or the desired length.

Continue circular knitting, and alternate these decreases until there are 32 st left:

Rnd 1: Continue with pattern until there are 3 st remaining. K2tog, K1.

Rnd 2: Continue with pattern until there are 3 st remaining. K1, K2tog.

Repeat these 2 sections, until there are 32 st left. Sew the toe together using the kitchener's stitch, as shown on page 89, and tie off the ends.

The Tulip

Lay out the two colors of wool in two piles with two crossways patterns each. The pieces should each measure about 4" x 8" (10 x 20 cm). Felt the wool, and let it dry. Cut out two red tulips and two each of the big and little green leaves as shown in the pattern on this page.

Sew the tulips on with loose basting stitches. Use the scraps of yarn from the knitting for the stitching. Sew the leaves on using leftover yarn as well. Be careful not to stick the needle all the way through the felt in order to keep the stitches invisible on the surface.

Pattern for the Tulips

Tulips

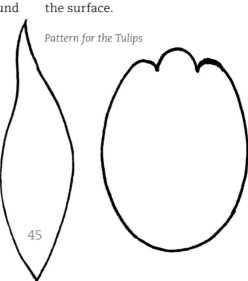

45

Aqua

Materials: 4 skeins Nuuk Løvegarn light blue-green # 66, green or white sewing thread, 1 oz. (30 g) white merino, a small amount of yellow wool.

Needles: Size 10 (U.K. size 6) double point needles

Gauge: 15 st x 19 rows stockinette stitch using size 10 needles = 4" X 4" (10 x 10 cm).

Size: The pattern is designed for size 6 ½-8 ½ (European size 37-39). You can alter the size by increasing or decreasing the length of the foot.

The Leg

On size 10 double point needles CO 36, and knit rounds on 4 needles in the following pattern:

Rnd 1: * P5, k1 in back of st *. Rep from * to * the entire round.

Rnd 2: * P5, k1 in back of st, p5, (k1, p1, k1, p1, k1 in the next stitch) *. Rep from * to * the entire round.

Rnd 3: * P5, k1 in back of st, p5, k5*. Rep from * to * the entire round.

Rnd 4: Same as 3rd round.

Rnd 5: * P5, k1 in back of st, p5, slip 1, k1, psso, k1, k2tog (knit 2 together)*. Rep from * to * the entire round.

Rnd 6: * P5, k1 in back of st, p5, k3 *. Rep from * to * the entire round.

Rnd 7: * P5, k1 in back of st, p5, slip 1, k2tog, psso *. Rep from * to * the entire round

Rnd 8: Same as 1st round.

Rnd 9: Same as 1st round.

Rnd 10: * P5, (k1, p1, k1, p1, k1 in the next stitch), p5, k1 in back of st *. Rep from * to * the entire round.

Rnd 11: * P5. k5, p5, k1 in back of st *. Rep from * to * the entire round.

Rnd 12: Same as 11th round.

Rnd 13: * P5, slip 1 st, k1, psso, k1, k2tog, p5, k1 in back of st *. Rep from * to * the entire round.

Rnd 14: * P5, k3, p5, k1 in back of st *. Rep from * to * the entire round.

Rnd 15: * P5, slip 1 st as if to k, k2tog, psso, p5, k1 in back of st *. Rep from * to * the entire round.

Rnd 16: Same as 1st round.

Knit 1-16 round a total of two times. Knit 7 rounds of * p11, k1 in back of st*. Rep from * to * the entire round. P 17 rounds.

The Heel

Let one of the stitches passed in the back of another stitch serve as the heel's center st. Put 7 stitches on either side of this stitch on a needle so that the heel can be knit using these 15 stitches.

Wrap and turn (w & t): Pull the yarn around to the front side of the work, transfer the next stitch onto the right needle, move the yarn to the back side of the work, and put the stitch back onto the left needle. Turn. You are now ready to knit the next row.

Purl up to and including the row with the stitches for the heel, w & t, k11, w & t, p7, w & t, k11, w & t, purl

1 round.* Knit from * to * a total of 5 times.

The Foot
Divide the stitches as they were before you began to work the heel. Purl 5.5" (13.5 cm).

The Toe
Rnd 1: Needle 1: P to last 3 st, p2 in back of st, p1. Needle 2: p1, p2 in back of st, p3. Needle 3: repeat as for needle 1. Needle 4: repeat as for needle 2.
Rnd 2: P.
Repeat these 2 rounds a total of four times. Sew the toe together on the wrong side using the kitchener's stitch, as shown on page 89, and tie off the ends.

Water Lily
Felt the material for the water lily as shown on page 19.

Aqua

Knitted slippers

Springtime

Materials: 2 skeins Cosy Wool Løvegarn light blue # 66, 1 skein Cosy Wool Løvegarn green #71.
Needles: Size 6 (U.K. 4); two large safety pins or stitch holders.
Gauge: 19 st x 36 rows of seed stitch on size 6 needles = 4" X 4" (10 x 10 cm).
Size: One size. The seed stitch is very flexible, and you can determine for yourself the length of the piece.

This design is rather wide, so if you have narrow feet, it would be a good idea to cast on fewer blue stitches (for the seed stitching). You can make the ankle narrower by knitting 45 rows when you start instead of 54. This way you will have 2 1/2 leaves on the top edge and can continue with the third leaf when you knit the slippers's inner heel.

Right foot

Begin by knitting the slipper's outer side from the heel. CO 6 stitches with the green yarn and 27 with the light blue. Knit the seed stitch with the blue stitches and the leafy edging with the green. See page 16 for seed stitching instructions, and the leafy edging pattern below. Remember to twist the two colors together when you change colors so that the edging and the foot are attached.

Knit 54 rows. Knit 23 stitches of seed st on the next needle (on the right side), and then cast on 22 more stitches in blue yarn. Put the remaining stitches on a stitch holder as shown in figure 2 on page 50. Continue with the seed st for the next 45 st that are now on the needle. When you reach a point that is 1.25" (3 cm) shorter than your foot, decrease 1 stitch on each side in each row until there are 27 stitches left. K 13 st, and break the yarn off, leaving a tail of 24" (60 cm). Put the stitches onto a stitch holder.

Now you will knit the slipper's inner heel. Go back to the point at which you cast the 22 stitches on, as shown in figure 3 on page 50. Gather 23 loops from the right side of the work. Knit 1 row of p1 in back of st using the loops, alternating 1 blue and 1 green st from the center of the slipper towards the sole. Cut the green yarn. K 1 row with blue yarn. Now add the stitches you put on the stich holder back onto the needle. Knit seed stitch over the blue stitches and leafy edge over the green. Continue with an additional 53 rows seed stitch and leafy edge. Bind off.

The right foot's leafy edge

Row 1: K3, yo, k1, yo, k2.
Row 2: P,6, inc 1 st, k1.
Row 3: K2, p1, k2, yo, k1, yo, k3.
Row 4: P8, inc 1 st, k2.
Row 5: K2, p2, k3, yo, k1, yo, k4.

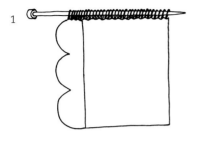

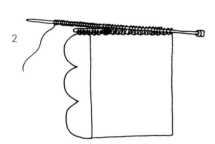

Row 6: P10, inc 1 st, k3.

Row 7: K2, p3, k4, yo, k1, yo, k5.

Row 8: P12, inc 1 st, k4.

Row 9: K2, p4, slip 1 stitch as if to k, k1, psso, k7, k2tog, k1.

Row 10: P10, inc 1 st, k5.

Row 11: K2, p5, slip 1 stitch as if to k, k1, psso, k5, k2tog, k1.

Row 12: P8, inc 1 st, k2, p1, k3.

Row 13: K2, p1, k1, p4, slip 1 stitch as if to k, k1, psso, k3, k2tog, k1.

Row 14: P6, inc 1 st, k3, p1, k3.

Row 15: K2, p1, k1, p5, slip 1 st, k1, psso, k1, k2tog, k1.

Row 16: P4, inc 1 st, k4, p1, k3.

Row 17: K2, p1, k1, p6, slip 1 st as if to k, k2tog, psso, k1.

Row 18: P2tog, bind 5 st off in p (p2tog stitch is the first stitch to be drawn over) k1, p1, k3. There are now 6 st left on the needle once again. Knit these 18 rows a total of six times to form the leafy edge.

Left foot

CO 27 with the blue yarn and 6 with the green. Knit as directed above for the right foot, but with the following changes:

· Remember to make the leafy edge for the left foot.

· When it comes time to cast the 22 st on, do not first knit 23 st. Use the blue yarn instead, and put the green st + 4 blue st onto a stitch holder right away. Then use the blue yarn to cast on the 22 stitches.

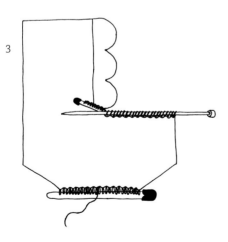

These drawings show how Springtime is to be knit

• When you have gathered the 23 loops for the inside of the heel, knit the blue and green stitches from the sole towards the center. Put the stitches from the stitch holder onto the needle. The next row is knit in leafy edge, 4 st seed st and the rest blue k. Continue after that with seed st and leafy edge pattern.

The left foot's leafy edge

Row 1: K2, yo, k1, yo, k3.
Row 2: K1, inc (increase) 1 st, k1, p6.
Row 3: K3, yo, k1, yo, k2, p1, k2.
Row 4: K2, inc 1 st, p8.
Row 5: K4, yo, k1, yo, k3, p2, k2.
Row 6: K3, inc 1 st, p10.
Row 7: K5, yo, 3 p, yo, k4, p3, k2.
Row 8: K4, inc 1 st, p12.
Row 9: K1, k2tog in back of st, k8, (slip st to left needle, pass 1 st over, slip st to right needle), p4, 2k.
Row 10: K5, inc 1 st, p10.
Row 11: K1, k2tog in back of st, k6, (slip st to left needle, pass 1 st over, slip st to right needle), p5, k2.
Row 12: K3, p1, k2, inc 1 st, p8.
Row 13: K1, k2tog in back of st, k4, (slip st to left needle, pass 1 st over, slip st to right needle), p4, k1, p1, k2.
Row 14: K3, p1, k 3, inc 1 st, p6.
Row 15: K1, k2tog in back of st, k2, (slip st to left needle, pass 1 st over, slip st to right needle), p5, k1, p1, k2.
Row 16: K3, p1, k4 , inc 1 st, p4.

Row 17: K1, k2tog in back of st, (slip st to left needle, pass 1 st over, slip st to right needle), p6, k1, p1, k2.
Row 18: K3 k, p1 p, k2 k. Bind off the last stitches. Work the last 2 stitches p2tog before psso (passing the previous stitch over).
Knit these 18 rows a total of six times to form the leafy edge.

Assembly

Divide the toe's stitches onto two needles, and use a yarn remnant to sew them together using the kitchener's stitch, as shown on page 89. Continue to sew the bottom of the slipper and the heel together using the mattress stitch, as shown on page 89. Sew the leafy edge together using green yarn. Weave in the ends.

TIP! This design doesn't have soles, but if you want to make them more skid-resistant, you can put liquid latex on the soles as shown on page 90.

Greek

(Note: sock pattern not included)
Materials: 1 skein Cosy Wool Løvegarn yellow # 22, 1 skein Cosy Wool Løvegarn light blue #66, liquid latex, cardboard.
Needle: Size 3, 16" (40 cm) circular needle
Gauge: 21 st x 42 rows seed stitch on size 3 needle = 4" X 4" (10 x 10 cm).
Size: This style is very elastic, and will fit sizes 6-7 ½ (European size 36-38). You can make it larger or smaller by adjusting the stitch count in the beginning. If you have a wide foot, you can knit more rounds of seed stitch than is specified in the pattern.

CO 89 onto a size 3, 16" circular needle using the yellow yarn. Make sure that you have a piece of yarn at least 27.5" (70 cm) long left once you have cast on, as you will need this to sew the sole together. Knit 30 rows of seed stitch, as shown on page 16, followed by 3 rows of p. Bind off securely.

Pattern for Pompons

Assembly

Sew the sole together using the kitchener's stitch as shown on page 89. When you have about 2.5" (6 cm) to go, fold the seams together so that they form a T, which is perpendicular to the stitching you have already done, as in the diagram. Stitch, then bind off securely.

The soles are sewn together in a T formation

Make two pompons, as shown on page 89, using the pattern below, and sew them on. Put a thin plastic bag over your foot, put the slipper on, and put a coat of liquid latex on the sole while the slipper is stretched. Keep the slipper on until the liquid latex has dried a bit. Repeat this process.

Greek

Heartwarmers

Heartwarmers

Materials: 3 skeins Nuuk Løvegarn raw white # 30, 2" X 4.5" (5 x 12 cm) red leather, white sewing thread, 50 glass beads in 2 mm size (black or bloodstone).

Needles: Sizes 8 and 10 ½ (U.K. sizes 5 & 7) double point needles

Gauge: 13 st x 18 rows of stockinette stitch on size 10 ½ needles = 4" X 4" (10 x 10 cm).

Size: The pattern is designed for shoe sizes 6 ½-8 ½ (European size 37-39). You can alter the size by increasing or decreasing the length of the foot.

The Leg

With size 10 ½ double point needles CO 40.

Rnd 1: P.

Cut out 10 little leather hearts using this pattern

Rnd 2: Cut 100" (2 1/2 meters) of sewing thread, and knit it in this manner: * 8 p, then put 5 beads and 1 leather heart onto the sewing thread using a needle, and push them all the way up to the work, then insert the needle back into the beads *. Repeat from * to * the entire round. Clip off some of the sewing thread, but knit the end in during the following three rounds so that it will be well attached.

Rnd 3: * P1, k6, p1*. Rep from * to * the entire round.

Rnd 4: * K1, p1, k4, p1, p1*. Rep from * to * the entire round.

Rnd 5: * K2, p1, k2, p1, k2*. Rep from * to * the entire round.

Rnd 6: * K3, p2, k3*. Rep from * to * the entire round.

Rnd 7: * K2, p1, k2, p1,k 2*. Rep from * to * the entire round.

Rnd 8: * K1, p1, k4, p, k1*. Rep from * to * the entire round.

Knit rows 3-8 a total of three times. Repeat the third row. Switch to size 8 double point needles and knit rib (k1, p1) while dec to 32 st in the following manner: * Knit 3 st, k2tog*, repeat from * to * the entire round. Knit the outermost 12 rows in rib (k1, p1).

The Heel

Put the st from needles 1 and 4 onto one needle. Switch to a size 10 ½ double point needles, and knit stockinette for 14 rows. Slip the 1st st off in each row.

Decrease for the heel as described below. Begin the dec on the back (wrong) side of the work.

P until there are 7 st left on the needle: p2tog, w & t (see page 46 for instructions).

K until there are 7 st left on the needle: k2tog in back of st, w & t.

P until there are 5 st left on the needle: p2tog, w & t.

K until there are 5 st left on the needle: k2tog in back of st, w & t.

P until there are 3 st left on the needle: p2tog, w & t.

K until there are 3 st left on the needle: k2tog in back of st, w & t.

Divide the st from the heel's needle onto two needles, and pick up 7 st along the sides of the heel. The new stitches are k into the back of st for the first round, and after that just k. The last two st in the first needle and the first two st of the 4th needle are k2tog every other round, until there are 32 st in the round.

The Foot

K the 1st and 4th needle (the sole) and continue the pattern in the 2nd and 3rd needle (top of the foot), as shown below. Continue in this manner up to 1" (2.5 cm) from the end of your foot.

Pattern Stitch

Row 1 (2nd & 3rd needle): K2, p1, k2 , p1, k4, p1, k2, p1, k2.

Row 2 (2nd & 3rd needle): K1, p1, k4 , p1, k2, p1, k4, p1, k1.

Row 3 (2nd & 3rd needle): P1, k6 , p2, k6, p1.

Row 4 (2nd & 3rd needle): K1, p1, k4, p1, k2, p1, k4 r, p1, k1.

Row 5 (2nd & 3rd needle): K2, p1, k2, p1, k4, p1, k2, p1, k2.

Row 6 (2nd & 3rd needle): K3, p2 , k6, p2, k3.

The Toe

Decrease as follows:

Rnd 1:

Row 1: 1st needle: k until there are 3 st left on the needle, k2tog, k1.

Row 2: K1, k2tog, follow pattern stitch.

Row 3: Pattern stitch, until there are 3 st left on the needle, k2tog, k1.

Row 4: K1, k2tog, k rest of row.

Rdn 2:

1st and 4th row; k. 2nd and 3rd row; pattern stitch.

Repeat these 2 rounds, until there are 20 st in the round. Sew the toe together using the kitchener's stitch, as shown on page 89, and tie the ends off securely.

Soft Skies

Materials: 1 skein Fonty Angora light blue # 338, 2 buttons, light blue sewing thread.
Needles: Sizes 0 and 4 (U.K. 2 & 3 ½)
Gauge: 13 st x 27 rows of k on size 4 needle = 2" X 2" (5 X 5 cm)
Size: Girls's sizes 8 – 8 ½ (European size 25-26)

The yarn used for this style is very soft, but not very sturdy, so I wouldn't recommend it for older children. If you want to make these slippers smaller, you can felt them, as shown on page 16.

Using size 0 needles CO 39. Switch to size 4 and knit as follows:

Row 1: P1, * k2, p 2*. Rep from * to *, until there are 26 st left, k the rest of the row.
Row 2: K25, p1, * k2, p2*. Rep from * to * the rest of the row.
Row 3: P1, *k 2, p2*. Rep from * to * until there are 24 st left, k the rest of the row.
Row 4: K23, k1, * p2, k2*. Rep from * to * the rest of the row.

The ribbed section stretches to form the front and bottom of the slipper when the foot is inserted. Continue in this manner, replacing 1k with 1 rib stitch in every row until all the st are rib st. After that, re-

Soft Skies

place rib st with knit st, until there are 13 rib st left. Bind off using the size 0 needle.

Assembly

Sew the slipper together in the front and back using the mattress stitch as shown on page 89. Make sure that 3 k st are in the front.

Left ankle strap

On size 4 needles CO 26, gather 6 st up in the center back of the slipper and CO an additional 10 st for a total of 42.

Row 1-2: K.

Row 3: K1, inc 1, k until there are 2 st left, inc 1, k1.

Row 4: K39, close off the next two st (buttonhole), k rest of row.

Row 5: K, cast 2 st on over the buttonhole.

Row 6: K1, k2tog, k until there are 3 st left, k2tog into back of st, k1.

Row 7-8: K.

Bind off.

Right ankle strap

On size 4 needle CO 10, gather 6 st up in the center back of the slipper and CO an additional 26 st for a total of 42.

Knit in the same manner as the left strap except for the 4th row, which is worked as follows: k2, bind off the next 2 st, k rest of row.

Weave in the ends and sew the buttons onto the straps.

My Shoes

Materials: 1 skein mercerized Løve Cotton 8/4 lavender # 81, about 700 small light lavender glass seed beads, 2 small buttons, and liquid latex (optional)

Needles: Size 0 (U.K. size 2)

Gauge: 19 st x 27 rows of stockinette on size 0 needles = 2" X 2" (5 X 5 cm)

Size: 9-12 months

This design is worked in stockinette stitch with beads. The right and left shoe begin the same, but they each have their own set of instructions. The soles are knit first in stockinette without beads.

The Sole

CO 34 st.

Row 1: P.

Row 2: K1, inc 1, k until there are 2 st left. Inc 1, k1.

Repeat these two rows until there are a total of 42 st on the needle. K 9 rows in stockinette.

Row 1: K1, k2tog, k until there are 3 st left on the needle. Knit k2tog into back of st, k1.

Row 2: P.

Repeat these two rows until there are 34 st on the needle. CO 8 new st so that there are a total of 42 st.

Knitting with beads

Knit one bead into every other stitch in the following manner: Push a bead close up against the work. Knit the stitch, making certain that the bead is picked up in the stitch and is placed close down on the right side of the work. Make sure that the bead stays in place and doesn't wander over to the wrong side of the work. This is especially important when you knit a row that contains beads.

Row 1: * K1, k1 with bead*. Rep from * to * the entire row.

Row 2: P.

Row 3: * K1 with bead, k1*. Rep from * to * the entire row.

Row 4: P.

The Uppers

Wax the end of the yarn, and string 350 beads onto it as shown on page 90. Knit the 8 new st without beads the first time, and after that knit with beads in every st, following the pattern below.

Right side of work row: k2, k with beads until there are two st left on the needle: k2

Wrong side of work row: p1, inc 1, p the rest of the row.

Repeat the rows above until there are 48 st on the needle. And then continue as follows:

Right shoe

Row 1: K17, k2 with beads, k10, knit with beads until there are two st left in the row, k2.

Row 2: P19, k10, p2, k17.

Row 3: Bind off 15 st (there is now 1 st on the right-hand needle), k1, knit 2 st with beads, k2 (these 6 st are for the strap) bind off the next 6 st, k1,

knit with beads until there are 2 st left, k2.

Row 4: P19, k2, put the 6 st for the strap on a safety pin or stitch holder.

Row 5: K2, knit with beads until there are two st left in the row, k2.

Knit rows 4 and 5 a total of 7 times = 17 rows.

Row 18: P19, k2, cast on 27 st.

Row 19: K29, knit with beads until there are two st left in the row, k2.

Row 20: P19, k rest of row.

Row 21: Same as row 19.

Row 22: P1, p2tog, p rest of row.

Row 23: K2, knit with beads until there are two st left in the row, k2.

Repeat rows 22 & 23 until there are 42 st in the row. P one row. Bind off 8 st and put the rest of the st on a large safety pin or a stitch holder.

Right strap

Knit the strap using 6 of the st on the safety pin or stitch holder:

Row 1: K2, p2, k2.

Row 2: K2, knit 2 st with beads, k2.

Repeat these two rows until there are a total of 29 rows.

Row 30: K4, pass 1 knit st over (pkso), k1, pkso, k1.

Row 31: K2, cast on 2 additional stitches, k2.

Row 32: K.

Row 33: K2, p2, k2.

Row 34: K2tog, k2, k2 into back of st. Bind off.

Left strap

CO 4 st onto size 0 needle.

Row 1: P.
Row 2: Inc 1, k2, inc 1.
Row 3: K2, p2, k2.
Row 4: K.
Row 5: K2, p2, pass 1 purl st over, k1, pkso, k1.
Row 6: K2, CO 2 st, k2.
Row 7: K2, 2p, k2.
Row 8: K2 , knit 2 st with beads, k2.
Repeat rows 7 and 8 until there are a total of 36 rows. Put the st on a safety pin or stitch holder.

Left shoe
Row 1: K29, knit with beads, until there are 2 st left, k2.
Row 2: P19, k29.
Row 3: Bind 27 st off, 1 r, knit with beads, until there are 2 st left, k2.
Row 4: P19, k2.
Row 5: K2, knit with beads until there are 2 st left, k2.
Knit rows 4 & 5 a total of 7 times = 17 rows.
Row 18: P19, k2, cast on 6 st. Include the 6 st from the strap (k2, p2, k2)

and cast on an additional 15 st.
Row 19: K17, knit 2 st with beads, k10, knit with beads, until there are 2 st left, k2.
Row 20: P19, k10, p2, k17.
Row 21: Same as row 19.
Row 22: P1, p2tog, p rest of row.
Row 23: K2, knit with beads, until there are 2 st left, k2.
Repeat rows 22 and 23 until there are 42 st in the row. P one row. Bind off 8 st and put the rest of the st on a large safety pin or stitch holder.

Assembly
Sew the heel seam together using the mattress stitch shown on page 89. Use this stitch to sew on the heel and toe. Remember to hold the upper part of the slipper tightly against to the sole as you stitch the front of the foot, as the upper is slightly longer than the sole in this section. Sew the side seam together using the kitchener's stitch, as shown on page 89. Sew on the buttons.

My Shoes

Crocheted slippers

Strawberry-colored Summer Slippers

Materials: 3 skeins Hjerte Blend pink # 434, 1 skein Hjerte Blend red # 4500, about 250 red 1.5-2 mm glass beads, red sewing thread, liquid latex, 9 oz. (3.5 mm) sole leather, signal red leather dye, colorless edge finish, 2 buttons or fancy beads, such as painted wooden beads.
Crochet hook: Size B1 (U.K. size 2)
Crochet gauge: 12 sc x 14 rows with two strands of yarn and a size B1 crochet hook = 2" X 2" (5 X 5 cm)
Size: Shoe sizes 6-6 ½ (European size 36-37), see page 92.

Altering the Size
You can alter the size by adding to or subtracting from the increases in the heel and front of the foot. You can of course also make the slippers longer or shorter depending on the length of your own foot.

The arch of the foot can also be made longer or shorter. Be sure to try to slipper on frequently as you are crocheting.

Crochet the whole slipper using 2 strands of yarn together.

The Heel
With pink yarn chain 11 crochet around the foundation row.
Rnd 1: 9 sc, crochet 3 sc in the next st. Crochet 8 sc on the underside of the foundation row, and crochet 2 sc in the next st.
Rnd 2: Inc 1 sc in every 2nd st the entire round.
Rnd 3: Sc.
Rnd 4: Sc, inc 2 sc evenly distributed throughout the round.

Strawberry-colored Summer Slippers

Repeat rnd 4, until the heel measures 2.75"–3.25" (7-8 cm), depending on what fits your foot. Remember to distribute the decreases at uneven intervals from round to round. Exert even pressure on the heel while you do this, so that the cotton yarn is stretched as much as possible.

Crochet the ankle strap out over 5 sc. Crochet back and forth, and turn every row with ch 1 until the strap measures 1.5" to 1.75" (4-4.5 cm). Bend the strap down, and crochet it onto the inside of the heel with 5 sl st. Break the yarn.

The Upper
With pink yarn ch 11 and crochet all the way around the foundation row.
Rnd 1: 9 sc, crochet 3 sc in the next st. Crochet 8 sc on the underside of the foundation row, and crochet 2 sc in the next st.
Rnd 2: Sc, inc 2 sc evenly throughout the round.

Repeat rnd 2, until the front of the foot measures about 2" (5 cm). Remember to distribute the decreases at uneven intervals. Crochet just until the work measures 3.75" (9.5 cm). Continue with the arch of the foot. This section connects the front of the foot with the heel, and should be about 3.25" (8 cm) long. Crochet this section back and forth over 20 st. Turn with ch 1. Crochet the next 8 rows with red yarn. When you crochet the last row of this section, you should crochet it together with the heel.

Sew beads on evenly distributed over the front of the slippers.

Edging
Cut a 6.5' (2 m.) length of red yarn. Separate two strands of the yarn and wax them lightly to give them more strength, then put about 70 red glass beads onto these strands as shown on page 90. Work sc around from the inner side of the slipper. On the front of the foot and the heel, put on one bead each time you crochet a sc. The beads should be put in place when you have put the hook through the work, right before you take hold of the yarn and pull the hook back.

Strap
Ch 81. Crochet all the way around the foundation row.
Rnd 1: Crochet 10 sc, ch 3. Skip 2 st, and crochet 66 sc. Crochet 3 sc in the next stitch. Then continue on the underside of the foundation row: 78 sc, crochet 2 sc in the next st.
Rnd 2: 81 sc, break the yarn, and weave in the end.

Assembly
Sew a bead or button onto the strap, and put it through the ankle strap. Cut out two leather soles using the pattern on page 92, or trace your own foot if you have altered the pattern's size. Apply the red leather dye and colorless edge finish on the edges of the soles as shown on page 91, and let them dry. Glue the soles on using liquid latex as shown on page 91.

Mouse

Materials: Cosy Wool Løvegarn: 1 skein light blue # 51, 1 skein beige # 32 (or a light brown yarn remnant), 1 skein pink # 12 (or a pink yarn remnant), a little bit of dark blue wool, 2" X 4" (5 x 10 cm) white felt, white DMC embroidery floss, dark blue DMC embroidery floss, liquid latex.

Crochet Hook: Sizes B1 (U.K. size 2) & E/4 (U.K. size 3½)

Gauge: 12 sc x 13 row with a size B1 crochet hook = 2" X 2" (5 X 5 cm)

Size: This pattern is designed for girl's shoe sizes 7–8 (European size 24-25). It is relatively narrow.

Altering the Size

You can alter the length of the foot by adding or subtracting ch 2-3 at the start for every ½" (1 cm) that your foot is longer or shorter than the size given.

Narrower foot: If you like you can skip the 4th round. If it is only the front of your foot that is narrower, you can skip the 5th round.

Wider foot: Repeat 1st round. If you like, crochet until the 9th round is completely finished, and then crochet another round up to the 20th st before your ls (last stitch).

When you alter the slipper's size, you should try it on frequently. You may need to also alter the part that fits over the top of the foot. You can do this by adjusting the number of ch you create in the chain for the top of the slipper.

The Sole

With size B1 crochet hook and light blue yarn ch 31 and sc in the 2nd ch from hook and in each additional ch on both sides of the foundation row.

Rnd 1: 29 sc, 3 sc in the next st. Put a red marking thread in the 2nd of the 3 stitches you have just crocheted. This is your first stitch (fs). Continue on the underside of the foundation row: 28 sc, crochet 2 sc in the next st. Put a blue marking thread in the stitch you have just crocheted. This is your last stitch (ls).

In the following rounds sc as normal while increasing the in the indicated stitches.

Rnd 2: Heel: 1 inc; 1 inc; toe: 3 sc in the fs; Heel: 1 inc, 1 inc, 1 sc in the ls.

Rnd 3: Heel: 1 sc, 1 inc; toe: 1 inc, 1 sc, 1 inc, 1 sc, 1 inc, 1 sc, 1 inc; Heel: 1 inc, 1 sc, 1 sc in the ls.

Rnd 4: Heel: 1 sc, 1 inc; toe: 1 inc, 11 sc, 1 inc; Heel: 1 inc, 1 sc, 1 sc in the ls. Drop yarn until round 6.

Rnd 5: This is a half round, which is crocheted on the top of the foot. Start in the 15th st from the heel. Toe: 3 sc in the fs. Finish in the 15th st before the ls. Break the yarn.

Rnd 6: Pick up yarn from round 4. Heel: 3 sc, 1 inc; toe: 1 inc, 1 sc, 1 inc, 1 sc, 1 inc, 1 sc, 1 inc; Heel: 1 inc, 3 sc, 1 sc in the ls. Drop yarn until round 8.

Rnd 7: This is a half round. Start in the 18th st from the ls. Toe: 1 inc, 21

Mouse

sc, 1 inc. Finish in the 18th st before the ls. Break the yarn.

Rnd 8: Pick up yarn from round 6. Heel: 1 sc, 1 inc; toe: 1 inc, 17 sc, 1 inc; Heel: 1 inc, 1 sc, 1 sc in the ls.

Rnd 9: Heel: 4 sc, 1 inc; toe: 1 inc, 5 sc, 1 inc; stop 20 st before the ls.

The Upper

Switch to a size E4 crochet hook. Ch 19, and attach these with 2 sl st to the opposite side of the sole. Note that the upper is crocheted in sl st in order to connect this section of the slipper to the sole. These stitches should remain unworked.

Rows 1, 3, 5, 9, 13 and 17: Sc, 2 sl st in the sole, turn.

Rows 7 and 15: Sc, crochet the last sc2tog, 2 sl st in the sole, turn.

Rows 11 and 19: Crochet the first sc-2tog, sc, 2 sl st in the sole, turn.

Rows 21, 23, and 25: Sc, sc2tog at the beginning and end of the row.

All of the even rows to and including the 24th row: Loop stitch (lp st) around a pencil with 1 sc between the loops, 2 sl st in the sole, turn. Read about loop stitching on page 18.

Row 26: Sc2tog the entire row. Continue in this manner on the sole, so that you are in fact crocheting in a ring.

Row 27: Put the crochet hook into the first stitch on the slipper's upper, yo, and pull the crochet hook out again. Repeat this for the rest of the st on the upper, yo, and pull the crochet hook through all the loops at once. Break the yarn and weave in the ends.

Ears

With size E4 crochet hook and pink yarn ch 3. Join with a sl st in 1 ch to form a ring.

Rnd 1: Ch 1, 7 sc in a ring.

Rnd 2: Ch 1, 2 sc in each st; around. Break the yarn.

Crochet another circle with the light blue yarn. Then crochet the 2 circles together using the light blue yarn. Work sc through both circles, break the yarn, and use a piece of the light blue yarn to sew the ears on. Weave in the ends.

Eyes

Cut out the four eyes from the white felt using the pattern on this page. Felt two small, hard balls (about ½" (1 cm.) in diameter) using the scrap of dark blue wool. Cut them in half using a sharp pair of scissors. Sew the eyes on using the button-hole stitch as shown on page 89. Use white embroidery floss for the white part of the eye and dark blue for the blue part.

Nose (Snout)

Embroider the mouse's nose using pink yarn and close satin stitches, as shown on page 89.

Pattern for the eyes

Hedgehog

Materials: 2 skeins Highland Løveg-arn brown # 110, Cosy Wool Løveg-arn: 1 skein beige # 32 or a scrap of light brown yarn and 1 skein light blue # 51 or a scrap of light blue yarn, red DMC embroidery floss, 4 black 4-5 mm glass beads, about 292 amber colored 3 mm glass beads, liquid latex.
Crochet hooks: Size B1 (U.K. size 2) & D3 (U.K. size 3), and a thick pencil for the loop stitches
Gauge: 13 sc x 13 rows with size B1 crochet hook = 2" X 2" (5 X 5 cm).
Size: Girl's shoe sizes 7-8 (European size 24 25)

Altering the Size

This design results in a narrow slip-per. The length can be altered by adding or subtracting 2-3 ch when you begin the work for every ½" (1 cm) that your foot is longer or short-er than the size given.

Narrower foot: If you want, skip the 4th round. If it is only the front of your foot that is narrower, you can skip the 5th round.

Wider foot: Repeat round 1. If you like, crochet until the 9th round is completely finished, and then cro-chet another round up to the 20th st before your ls (last stitch). Remem-ber to mark the last stich in the pat-tern to insure you are stopping at the correct stitch.

When you alter the slipper's size, you should try it on frequently. You may need to also alter the part that fits over the top of the foot. You can do this by adjusting the number of ch you create for the top of the slip-per. It will also mean that you will need to crochet fewer rows than the 10 I specify where the two heels sec-tions come together.

The Sole

With brown yarn and size B1 crochet hook ch 31, sc in the 2nd ch from hook and in each additional ch on both sides of the foundation row.
Rnd 1: Sc in the first 29 sts, 3 sc in the next stitch. Put a red marking thread in the 2nd of the 3 stitches you have just crocheted. This is your fs (first stitch) or toe. Continue on the underside of the foundation row with: 28 sc, crochet 2 sc in the next stitch. Put a blue marking thread in the stitch you have just crocheted. This is your last stitch (ls) or heel.
In the following rounds sc as normal while increasing the in the indicated stitches.
Rnd 2: Heel: 1 inc, 1 inc; toe: 3 sc in the fs; Heel: 1 inc, 1 inc, 1 sc in the ls.
Rnd 3: Heel: 1 sc, 1 inc; toe: 1 inc, 1 sc, 1 inc, 1 sc, 1 inc, 1 sc, 1 inc; Heel: 1 inc, 1 sc, 1 sc in the ls.
Rnd 4: Heel: 1 sc, 1 inc; toe: 1 inc, 11 sc, 1 inc; Heel: 1 inc, 1 sc, 1 sc in the ls. Drop yarn until the 6th round.
Rnd 5: This is a half round, which is crocheted on the front part of the foot. With new yarn start at the 15th st from the ls. Toe: 3 sc in the fs. End

in the 15th st from the ls. Break the yarn.

Rnd 6: Pick up yarn from the 4th round. Heel: 3 sc, 1 inc ; toe: 1 inc, 1 sc, 1 inc, 1 sc, 1 inc, 1 sc, 1 inc; Heel: 1 inc, 3 sc, 1 sc in the ls. Drop yarn until the 8th round.

Rnd 7: This is a half round. With new yarn start in the 18th st from the ls. Toe: 1 inc, 21 sc, 1 inc. End in the 18th st from the ls. Break the yarn.

Rnd 8: Pick up yarn from the 6th round. Heel: 1 sc, 1 inc; toe: 1 inc, 17 sc, 1 inc; Heel: 1 inc, 1 sc, 1 sc in the ls.

Rnd 9: Heel: 4 sc, 1 inc; toe: 1 inc, 5 sc, 1 inc; stop 20 m before the ls.

The Upper

Switch to the size D3 crochet hook, and take up the other ball of yarn. Wax the end of the yarn and string 107 beads onto it, as shown on page 90. Use the loop from the sole, and crochet ch 13. Crochet back and forth over these ch. Crochet with the loop stitch around a thick pencil in every 2nd row with 3 sc between the loops, as described on page 18. Take on 1 bead per loop.

Note that the upper is crocheted in sl st in order to connect this section of the slipper to the sole. These stitches should remain unworked.

Row 1: Sc, 2 sl st in the sole, turn.
Row 2: 2 sc, lp st, turn with ch 1.
Row 3: Sc, 2 sl st in the sole, turn.
Row 4: Lp st, turn with ch 1.
Repeat these 4 rows a total of 6

times = 24 rows. Then crochet the first 3 rows again for a total of 27 rows.

Let the loop hang, and go back to the foundation row that you began the top of the slipper with. Now crochet on the other side, and continue until the slipper has a piece identical to the one you had just made. Use the first ball of yarn, and put 42 beads on it before you begin. Start near the sole:

Row 1: Sc, turn with ch 1.
Row 2: 3 sc, lp st, 2 sl st in the sole, turn.
Row 3: Sc, turn with ch 1.
Row 4: 1 sc, lp st, 2 sl st in the sole, turn.
Repeat these 4 rows a total of 6 times = 24 rows. Then crochet the first 3 rows again for a total of 27 rows. Break the yarn, and continue with the loop from before. Crochet over the st from both of the heel sections.
Row 1: Lp st, 2 sl st in the sole, turn.
Row 2: Sc, 2 sl st in the sole, turn.
Row 3: 2 sc, lp st, 2 sl st in the sole, turn.
Row 4: Sc, 2 sl st in the sole, turn.
Repeat these 4 rows a total of 2 times = 8 rows Then repeat the first 2 rows for a total of 10 rows.
Continue as follows:
Row 1: Crochet the first sc2tog, 2 sc, lp st, crochet the last sc2tog, 2 sl st in the sole, turn.
Row 2: Sc, 2 sl st in the sole, turn.
Row 3: Crochet the first sc2tog, and

begin again with lp st, at the same time as you insert the crochet hook in the 2nd stitch, lp st. Crochet the last 2 sc together, 2 sl st in the sole, turn.

Row 4: Sc, 2 sl st in the sole, turn.

Row 5: Crochet the first sc2tog, 1 sc, lp st. Crochet the last 2 sc together, 2 sl st in the sole, turn.

Row 6: Sc, dec 1 sc at the beginning and end of the row, 2 sl st in the sole. Switch to beige, and work sc in the round in which both the top of the slipper and sole are crocheted:

Row 1: Sc.

Row 2: Crochet the first sc2tog all the way across to the end of the uppers, then work sc in the st of the sole.

Repeat these rounds = a total of 4 rounds. Next crochet 2 round sc, and 1 round, in which you crochet sc2tog all the way around. Switch to brown yarn, and crochet 2 rounds sc. Break the yarn, and weave in the ends.

Assembly

Sew the eyes on and embroider a little mouth using running stitches with overcasting, as shown on page 89. Crochet a round of sc on the uppermost edge using light blue yarn and a B1 crochet hook, bind off. Add the soles using liquid latex as shown on page 91.

Hedgehog

Summer Slippers

Materials: Cotmondo cotton 8/8: 1 skein light green # 71, 2 skein pink # 47, 2 mm glass beads: about 70 clear green and about 150 clear pink; green and pink sewing thread, 9 oz. (3.5 mm) sole leather, liquid latex.
Crochet Hook: Size B1 (U.K. size 2)
Gauge: 13 sc x 14 rows = 2" X 2" (5 X 5 cm).
Size: Shoe size 8 ½ (European size 39), see page 92.

Altering the Size

You can alter the length of the foot by adding or subtracting 2-3 ch at the start for every ½" (1 cm) that your foot is longer or shorter than the size given.

Narrower foot: If you like, you can skip the 2nd and 5th round. If it is only the front of your foot that is narrower, you can skip the 9th round.

Wider foot: Alter the sole from the 10th round as follows:

Summer Slippers

Rnd 11: Heel: 4 sc, 1 inc; toe: 1 inc, 13 sc, 1 inc; Heel: 1 inc, 4 sc, 1 sc in the ls.

Rnd 12: Heel: 2 sc, 1 inc; toe: 1 inc, 9 sc, 1 inc; Heel: 1 inc, 2 sc, 1 sc in the ls.

Rnd 13: 58 sc (or to the middle of the big toe when viewed from the side).

When you alter the slipper's size, you should try it on frequently. You may need to also alter the part that fits over the top of the foot. You can do this by adding to or subtracting from the increases in the top of the slipper's 3rd row, and by adjusting the number of rows you crochet in the top of the slipper.

The Sole

With green yarn and size B1 crochet hook ch 51, sc in the 2nd ch from hook and in each additional ch on both sides of the foundation row.

Rnd 1: 49 sc, 3 sc in the next st. Put a red marking thread in the 2nd of the 3 stitches you have just crocheted. This is your first stitch (fs). Continue on the underside of the foundation row with: 48 sc, crochet 2 sc in the next st. Put a blue marking thread in the stitch you have just crocheted. This is your last stitch (ls).

Rnd 2: Work sc up to your fs, 3 sc in the fs, Work sc to the ls, 3 sc in the ls. In the following rounds sc as normal while increasing the in the indicated stitches.

Rnd 3: Heel: 1 inc, 1 inc. Toe: 3 sc in the fs. Heel: 1 inc, 1 inc, 1 sc, 1 sc in the ls.

Rnd 4: Heel: 1 inc. Toe: 1 inc, 1 sc, 1 inc, 1 sc, 1 inc, 1 sc, 1 inc. Heel: 1 inc, 1 sc in the ls.

Rnd 5: Heel: 4 sc, 1 inc. Toe: 1 inc, 5 sc, 1 inc. Heel: 1 inc, 4 sc, 1 sc in the ls. Switch to the pink yarn.

Rnd 6: Heel: 1 sc, 1 inc. Toe: 1 inc, 11 sc, 1 inc. Heel: 1 inc, 1 sc, 1 sc in the ls. Drop yarn until round 8.

Rnd 7: This is a half round, which is crocheted on the front part of the foot. Start in the 19th st from the ls. Toe: 3 sc in the fs. Finish in the 19th st before the ls, break the yarn.

Rnd 8: Pick up yarn from round 6. Heel: 3 sc, 1 inc. Toe: 1 inc, 1 sc, 1 inc, 1 sc, 1 inc, 1 sc, 1 inc. Heel: 1 inc, 3 sc, 1 sc in the ls. Drop yarn until round 10.

Rnd 9: This is a half round. Start in the 34th st from the ls. Toe: 1 inc, 21 sc, 1 inc. Finish in the 34th st before the ls.

Rnd 10: Pick up yarn from round 8. Heel: 1 sc, 1 inc. Toe: 1 inc, 17 sc, 1 inc. Heel: 1 inc, 1 sc, 1 sc in the ls.

Rnd 11: 58 sc (or to the middle of the big toe when viewed from the side). Pull on the sole to stretch it to fit. Note that this sole is narrow, so the widest part of your foot will barely go ½" (1 cm) over the edges of the sole. Press the sole lightly with an iron so that it is flat. Lay it on a piece of paper and draw around it. This is the pattern you will use when you cut out your leather soles.

The Upper

Use the loops from the sole, and crochet ch 25. Attach them to the sole on the opposite side of the foot with 2 sl st, turn. Note that the upper is crocheted in sl st in order to connect this section of the slipper to the sole. These stitches should remain unworked.

Row 1: Sc, 2 sl st in the sole, turn.
Row 2: Sc, 2 sl st in the sole, turn.
Row 3: Sc, inc 2 sc evenly distributed throughout the row, 2 sl st in the sole, turn.

The above 3 rows are worked 5 times = 15 rows in all. They are then crocheted an additional 5 times in which there is only 1 sc inc in the 3rd row = 30 rows altogether. Try to distribute the increases evenly so that they are not noticeable. After the 21st, 24th and 27th row, 2 incomplete rows are crocheted as follows:

Row 1: Inc 1 sc, 9 sc, break the yarn. Go to the last 10 st in the row, 9 sc, inc 1 sc, 2 sl st in the sole, turn.
Row 2: 5 sc, break the yarn. Go to the last 5 st in the row, 5 sc, 2 sl st in the sole, turn. In the next row crochet over the ends (to include them).

End with a row of sc and 1 sl st in the sole, break the yarn and weave in the ends.

Stretch the upper until you like its shape and it fits your foot.

Stitch a heart of little light-green beads on the top of the slipper following the pattern on this page. Sew pink glass beads on the open edges.

Cut out two leather soles using the paper pattern you made earlier, and glue them on using liquid latex, as described on page 91.

Tulip-colored Slippers

Materials: Heavy Løvegarn: 2 skeins green # 72, 1 skein light green # 70, 1 skein red # 15, 1.5 mm glass beads (about 100 clear red and 70 clear green), green sewing thread, about 1 m thin metal wire, liquid latex, 9 oz. (3.5 mm) sole leather, green leather dye, colorless edge finish.
Crochet hook: Size D3 (U.K. size 3)
Gauge: 10 sc x 11 rows = 2" X 2" (5 X 5 cm) using size D3 crochet hook
Size: Shoe size 7 ½ (European size 38), see page 92.

Altering the Size

You can alter the length of the slipper by adding or subtracting 2 ch at the start for every ½" (1 cm) that your foot is longer or shorter than the size given.

Narrower foot: If you like, you can skip the 4th and 8th round. If it is only the front of your foot that is narrower, you can skip the 7th round.

Wider foot: Repeat 1st round. If you wish you can add the following round after the 9th round:
Heel: 2 sc, 1 inc. Toe: 1 inc, 9 sc, 1 inc. Heel: 1 inc, 2 sc, 1 sc in the ls.

When you alter the slipper's size, you should try it on frequently. You may need to also alter the part that fits over the top of the foot. You can do this by adjusting the number of ch you create for the top of the slipper, or by adding or subtracting decreases.

The Sole

With green yarn #72 and a D3 Hook ch 36, sc across.
Rnd 1: 34 sc, 3 sc in the next stitch. Put a red marking thread in the 2nd of the 3 stitches you have just crocheted. This is your first stitch (fs). Continue on the underside of the foundation row with: 33 sc, crochet 2 sc in the next stitch. Put a blue marking thread in the stitch you have just crocheted. This is your last stitch (ls).

In the following rounds sc as normal while increasing the in the indicated stitches.
Rnd 2: Heel: 1 inc, 1 inc. Toe: 3 sc in the fs. Heel: 1 inc, 1 inc, 1 sc in the ls.
Rnd 3: Heel: 1 sc, 1 inc. Toe: 1 inc, 1 sc, 1 inc, 1 sc, 1 inc, 1 sc, 1 inc. Heel: 1 inc, 1 sc, 1 sc in the ls.
Rnd 4: Heel: 1 sc, 1 inc. Toe: 1 inc, 11 sc, 1 inc. Heel: 1 inc, 1 sc, 1 sc in the ls. Drop yarn until round 6.
Rnd 5: This is a half round, which is crocheted on the front part of the foot. Start in the 18th st from the ls. Toe: 3 sc in the fs. Finish in the 18th st before the ls.
Rnd 6: Pick up yarn from round 4. Heel: 3 sc, 1 inc. Toe: 1 inc, 1 sc, 1 inc, 1 sc, 1 inc, 1 sc, 1 inc. Heel: 1 inc, 3 sc, 1 sc in the ls. Drop yarn until round 8.
Rnd 7: This is a half round. Start in the 22nd st from the ls. Toe: 1 inc, 21 sc, 1 inc. Finish in the 22nd st before the ls.
Rnd 8: Heel: 1 sc, 1 inc. Toe: 1 inc, 17 sc, 1 inc. Heel: 1 inc, 1 sc, 1 sc in the ls.
Rnd 9: Heel: 4 sc, 1 inc. Toe: 1 inc, 5 sc, 1 inc. Heel: 1 inc, 4 sc, 1 sc in the ls.
Rnd 10: 43 sc (or to the middle of the big toe when viewed from the side).

Press the sole with an iron so that it is flat. Lay it on a piece of paper and trace around it. This is the shape you will use when you cut out your leather soles.

The Uppers

Note that the upper is crocheted in sl st in order to connect this section of the slipper to the sole. These stitches should remain unworked.

Use the loops from the sole, and crochet ch 18. Attach them to the sole on the opposite side of the foot with 2 sl st, turn.
Rnd 1 (with green): Work sc in the ch, 2 sl st in the sole, turn.
Rnd 2: Sc, 2 sl st in the sole, turn.

Rnd 3 (with light green): Inc 1 sc in the first and last st, 2 sl st in the sole, turn.

Rnd 4: Sc, 2 sl st in the sole, turn.

Rnd 5 (with green): Inc 1 sc in the first and last st, 2 sl st in the sole, turn.

Rnd 6: Sc, 2 sl st in the sole, turn.

Rnd 7 (with light green): Inc 1 sc, 9 sc, turn.

Rnd 8: Skip the first st, sc, 2 sl st in the sole, turn.

Rnd 9 (with green): Inc 1 sc, 9 sc, turn.

Rnd 10: Skip the first st, sc, 2 sl st in the sole, turn.

Rnd 11 (with light green): Inc 1 sc, 8 sc, turn with 1 ch.

Rnd 12: Sc, 2 sl st in the sole, turn.

Rnd 13 (with green): Inc 1 sc, 9 sc, turn with 1 ch.

Rnd 14: Sc, 2 sl st in the sole, turn.

Rnd 15 (with light green): Inc 1 sc, 9 sc, inc 1 sc, 1 ch. Drop yarn until round 17.

Rnd 16 (with red): Start from the sole. 7 sc, break the yarn.

Rnd 17 (with light green): Pick up yarn from round 15. 2 sl st in the sole, turn.

Rnd 18 (with green): Inc 1 sc, 11 sc, inc 1 sc, break the yarn.

Now you will crochet the other side of the upper. Start in the 10th st

Tulip-colored Slippers

before the sole.

Rnd 1 (with light green): 9 sc, 1 inc, 2 sl st in the sole, turn.

Rnd 2 (with light green): Sc, crochet the last sc2tog, turn.

Rnd 3 (with green): 9 sc, 1 inc, 2 sl st in the sole, turn.

Rnd 4 (with green): Sc, crochet the last sc2tog, turn with 1 ch.

Rnd 5 (with light green): 8 sc, 1 inc, 2 sl st in the sole, turn.

Rnd 6 (with light green): Sc, turn with 1 ch.

Rnd 7 (with green): 9 sc, 1 inc, 2 sl st in the sole, turn.

Rnd 8 (with green): Sc, turn with 1 ch.

Rnd 9 (light green): 1 inc, 9 sc, 1 inc, 2 sl st in the sole. Switch to the red yarn.

Rnd 10 (with red): 7 sc, break the yarn.

Rnd 11 (with light green): Start from the sole. Sc, turn with 1 ch.

Rnd 12 (with green): 1 inc, 11 sc, 1 inc, 2 sl st in the sole, turn.

Now the upper part of the slipper is attached again:

Rnd 1 (with green): 15 sc, 2 ch, 15 sc, 2 sl st in the sole, turn.

Rnd 2 (with red): Sc in the first 9 sc, break the yarn. Sc in the last 9 sc, break the yarn.

Rnd 3 (with light green): Sc, 2 sl st in the sole, turn.

Rnd 4 (with light green): Sc, 2 sl st in the sole, turn.

Rnd 5 (with green): Sc, 2 sl st in the sole, turn.

Rnd 6 (with red): Sc in the first 11 sc, break the yarn. Sc in the last 11 sc, break the yarn.

Rnd 7 (with green): Sc, 1 sl st in the sole, break the yarn and weave in the ends.

Decoration

Ch 24 in light green, break the yarn, and create a wreath by sewing mattress stitches in the first ch. Lay this wreath over the hole on the top part of the slipper. This should conceal the rough edges of the hole. Attach the wreath with pins and sew on using green thread and the red glass beads. I have used 1 bead in every chain stitch.

Now take about 20" (50 cm) thin steel wire. Attach them to the hole using a crochet hook as shown, and pull the beads onto it. Tie off securely. Sew green beads around the edge of the large opening on the top of the slippers.

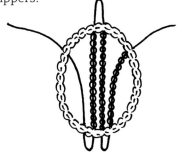

Cut out two soles using the paper pattern you made. Apply the green leather dye and colorless edge finish on the edges of the soles as shown on page 91. Glue the soles on using liquid latex as shown on page 91.

Knobby Boots

Materials: 7 skeins Cosy Wool Løvegarn light blue # 51, 1 skein Rustico Løvegarn citron yellow # 20, about 90 clear yellow 3 mm glass beads, yellow sewing thread, liquid latex.

Crochet Hooks: Sizes B1 (U.K. size 2) & D3 (U.K. size 3)

Gauge: 12 sc x 13 rows = 2" X 2" (5 X 5 cm) using a size B1 crochet hook

Size: This design is very generous in size and fits shoe sizes 6 ½-8 ½ (European size 37-39).

Altering the Size

You can alter the length of the foot by adding or subtracting 2-3 ch at the start for every ½" (1 cm) that your wish to shorten the size.

Narrower foot: If you like, you can skip the 2nd and 5th rounds. If it is only the front of your foot that is narrower, you can skip the 9th round.

Wider foot: Note that this design is already rather wide. If necessary, you can alter the pattern starting from round 12 as follows:

Rnd 13: Heel: 2 sc, 1 inc. Toe: 1 inc, 9 sc, 1 inc. Heel: 1 inc, 2 sc, 1 sc in the ls.

Rnd 14: Heel: 3 sc, 1 inc. Toe: 1 inc, 17 sc, 1 inc. Heel: 1 inc, 3 sc, 1 sc in the ls.

Rnds 15-17: Sc.

Rnd 18: Sc until 7 st after the fs, 2 sc.

Switch to the size D3 crochet hook, and turn. Make sure at this point that the work is right-side out.

When you alter the boot's size, you should try it on frequently. You may need to also alter the part that fits over the top of the foot. You can do this by adding to or subtracting from the increases as you work the top of the boot. Take care to still place the bobbles evenly starting at the center of the work.

One way to make the boot larger is to use a thicker crochet hook. This makes the work looser, but it can tolerate this because it is quite dense. You shouldn't, however, use a thinner crochet hook to make it smaller. That will make the crocheting too tight and difficult to work with.

Bobbles

Switch to the yellow yarn just before you pull the yarn through the two loops on the crochet hook as you crochet the last sc before the bobble. Crochet 5 hdc (half double crochet) in the next st. Now there are 6 loops on the crochet hook. Pull the blue yarn through the loops. Now you have a bobble. Let the yellow yarn follow along for the next bobble by crocheting over it with the blue yarn. If the bobble wants to extend out the back side of the work, push it to the right side with the crochet hook or or the top of a pencil. Break off the yellow yarn when the row is finished.

The Sole

The sole is crocheted in sc using a size B1 crochet hook.

Left foot: With light blue yarn ch 46. Sc around the foundation row.

Rnd 1: 44 sc, 3 sc in the next st. Put a red marking thread in the 2nd of the 3 stitches you have just crocheted. This is your first stitch (fs). Continue on the underside of the foundation row with: 43 sc, crochet 2 sc in the next stitch. Put a blue marking thread in the stitch you have just crocheted. This is your last stitch (ls).

Rnd 2: Work sc up to the fs, 3 sc in the fs. Work sc up to the ls, 3 sc in the ls.

In the following rounds sc as normal while increasing the in the indicated stitches.

Rnd 3: Heel: 1 inc, 1 inc. Toe: 3 sc in the fs. Heel: 1 inc, 1 inc, 1sc, 1 sc in the ls.

Rnd 4: Heel: 1 inc. Toe: 1 inc, 1 sc, 1 sc, 1 sc, 1 inc, 1 sc, 1 inc. Heel: 1 inc, 1 sc in the ls.

Rnd 5: Heel: 4 sc, 1 inc. Toe: 1 inc, 5 sc, 1 inc. Heel: 1 inc, 4 sc, 1 inc. Heel: 1 inc, 4 sc, 1 inc in the ls.

Rnd 6: Heel: 1 sc, 1 inc. Toe: 1 inc, 11 sc, 1 inc. Heel: 1 inc, 1 sc, 1 sc in the ls. Drop yarn until rnd 8.

Rnd 7: This is a half round, which is crocheted on the front part of the foot. Start in the 19th st from the ls.

Toe: 3 sc in the fs. Finish in the 35th st before the ls.

Rnd 8: Pick up yarn from rnd 6. Heel: 3 sc, 1 inc. Toe: 1 inc, 1 sc, 1 inc, 1 sc, 1 inc, 1 sc, 1 inc. Heel: 1 inc, 3 sc, 1 sc in the ls. Drop yarn until rnd 10.

Rnd 9: This is a half round. Start in 22nd st from the ls. Toe: 1 inc, 21 sc, 1 inc. Finish in the 38th st before the ls.

Rnd 10: Pick up yarn from rnd 8. Heel: 1 sc, 1 inc. Toe: 1 inc, 17 sc, 1 inc. Heel: 1 inc, 1 sc, 1 sc in the ls. Drop yarn until rnd 12.

Rnd 11: This is a half round. Start in the 31st st from the ls. Toe: 1 inc, 23 sc, 1 inc. Finish in the 40th st before the ls.

Rnd 12: Pick up yarn from rnd 10. Heel: 4 sc, 1 inc. Toe: 1 inc, 13 sc, 1 inc. Heel: 1 inc, 4 sc, 1 sc in the ls.

Rnds 13-15: Sc.

Rnd 16: Work sc up to and including the fs. Crochet an additional 7 sc, 2 sl st. Switch to a size D3 crochet hook, and turn. You are now ready to crochet the upper, so make certain that the right side of the work is turned out.

Right foot: Same as left, except for changes in the following rounds:

Rnd 7: This is a half round. Start in the 35th st from the ls. Toe: 3 sc in the fs. Finish in the 19th st before the ls.

Rnd 9: This is a half round. Start in the 38th st from the ls. Toe: 1 inc, 21 sc, 1 inc. Finish in the 22nd st before the ls.

Rnd 11: This is a half round. Start in the 40th st from the ls. Toe: 1 inc, 23 sc, 1 inc. Finish in the 31st st before the ls.

The Uppers

Note that sl st are crocheted to be used to attach the uppers to the soles. You should never crochet in these sl st.

Row 1: 15 sc, 2 sl st in the sole, turn.

Row 2: Sc, inc 1 sc on each end of the row, 2 sl st in the sole, turn.

Row 3 and all odd rows up to and including the 35th row: Sc, 2 sl st in the sole, turn.

Row 4: Inc 1 sc, 2 sc, bobble, 9 sc, bobble, 2 sc, inc 1 sc, 2 sl st in the sole, turn.

Row 6 & 8: Sc, inc 1 sc on each end of the row, 2 sl st in the sole, turn.

Row 10: Inc 1 sc, bobble, 9 sc, bobble, 9 sc, bobble, inc 1 sc, 2 sl st in the sole, turn.

Row 12 & 14: Sc, 2 sl st in the sole, turn.

Row 16: 7 sc, bobble, 9 sc, bobble, 7 sc, 2 sl st in the sole, turn.

Row 18: Sc, 2 sl st in the sole, turn.

Row 20, 24, 26, 30, 32, & 36 : Sc, inc 1 sc on each end of the row, 2 sl st in the sole, turn.

Row 22: Inc 1 sc, 2 sc, bobble, 9 sc, bobble, 9 sc, bobble, 2 sc, inc 1 sc, 2 sl st in the sole, turn.

Row 28: Inc 1 sc, bobble, 9 sc, bobble, 9 sc, bobble, 9 sc, bobble, inc 1 sc, 2 sl st in the sole, turn.

Row 34: Inc 1 sc, 8 sc, bobble, 9 sc, bobble, 9 sc, bobble, 8 sc, inc 1 sc, 2 sl st in the sole, turn.

Row 37: Sc (no sl st in the sole).

The Heel

The heel is crocheted back and forth along the heel section of the sole, and every row is attached to the upper with 2 sl st. Just continue by using 2 loops from the uppers. Remember the sl st should always remain unworked.

All odd rows from 1-17: Inc 1 sc on each side of the round, 2 sc in the upper, turn.

Row 2, 6, 8, 12, 14, & 18: Sc, 2 sl st in the upper, turn.

Row 4: 9 sc, bobble, 9 sc, bobble, 9 sc, bobble, 9 sc, bobble, 9 sc, 2 sl st in the upper, turn.

Row 10: 7 sc, bobble, 9 sc, bobble, 9 sc, bobble, 9 sc, bobble, 9 sc, bobble, 7 sc, 2 sl st in the upper, turn.

Row 16: 5 sc, bobble, 9 sc, bobble, 9 sc, bobble, 9 sc, bobble, 9 sc, bobble, 9 sc, bobble, 5 sc, 2 sl st in the upper, turn.

Break the yarn after the 18th row, start now with the ls to crochet the leg of the boot.

The Boot Shaft

The shaft of the boots is crocheted working back and forth in rows that start and end in the ls. It is turned with 1 ch after each row.

Row 1-3: Sc.

Row 4: Bobble, 9 sc, bobble, 9 sc, bobble, 9 sc, inc 1 sc, 1 sc, bobble, 9 sc, bobble, 1 sc, inc 1 sc, 9 sc, bobble, 9 sc, bobble, 9 sc, turn.

Row 5-9: Sc.

Row 10: 5 sc, bobble, 9 sc, bobble, 9 sc, bobble, 5 sc, inc 1 sc, 6 sc, bobble, 6 sc, inc 1 sc, 5 sc, bobble, 9 sc, bobble, 9 sc, bobble, 4 sc, turn.

Row 11-15: Sc.

Row 16: Bobble, 9 sc, bobble, 9 sc, bobble, 11 sc, inc 1 sc, 1 sc, bobble, 9 sc, bobble, 1 sc, inc 1 sc, 11 sc, bobble, 9 sc, bobble, 9 sc, turn.

Row 17-21: Sc.

Row 22: 5 sc, bobble, 9 sc, bobble, 9 sc, bobble, 7 sc, inc 1 sc, 6 sc, bobble, 6 sc, inc 1 sc, 7 f sc, bobble, 9 sc, bobble, 9 sc, bobble, 4 sc, turn.

Row 23-27: Sc.

Row 28: Bobble, 9 sc, bobble, 9 sc, bobble, 13 sc, inc 1 sc, 1 sc, bobble, 9 sc, bobble, 1 sc, inc 1 sc, 13 sc, bobble, 9 sc, bobble, 9 sc, turn.

Row 29-33: Sc.

Row 34: 5 sc, bobble, 9 sc, bobble, 9 sc, bobble, 9 sc, inc 1 sc, 6 sc, bobble, 6 sc, inc 1 sc, 9 sc, bobble, 9 sc, bobble, 9 sc, bobble, 4 sc, turn.

Row 35-39: Sc.

Row 40: Bobble, 9 sc, bobble, 9 sc, bobble, 15 sc, inc 1 sc, 1 sc, bobble, 9 sc, bobble, 1 sc, inc 1 sc, 15 sc, bobble, 9 sc, bobble, 9 sc, turn.

Row 41-45: Sc.

Row 46: 5 sc, bobble, 9 sc, bobble, 9 sc, bobble, 11 sc, inc 1 sc, 6 sc, bobble, 6 sc, inc 1 sc, 11 sc, bobble, 9 sc, bobble, 9 sc, bobble, 4 sc, turn.

Row 47-51: Sc.

Row 52: Bobble, 9 sc, bobble, 9 sc, bobble, 19 sc, bobble, 9 sc, bobble, 19 sc, bobble, 9 sc, bobble, 9 sc, turn.

Row 53-57: Sc.

Row 58: 5 sc, bobble, 9 sc, bobble, 9 sc, bobble, 19 sc, bobble, 19 sc, bobble, 9 sc, bobble, 9 sc, bobble, 4 sc, turn.

Row 59-63: Sc.

Row 64: Same as 52. row.

Row 65-69: Sc.

Row 70: Same as 58. row.

Row 71-75: Sc.

Row 76: Same as 52. row.

Row 77-81: Sc.

Cut the yarn so that the end measures about 20" (50 cm), and use this to sew the boot together with the ls. Stitch through the outermost loops, making sure the rows line up nicely.

Sew the beads on. If desired, make a braid measuring about 12" (30 cm) long using 9 threads of the blue yarn, and sew this onto the middle of the back of the boot.

Put the boots on, and draw around your foot with a piece of chalk. Give the soles you have just outlined 3 to 4 coats of liquid latex, as shown on page 90. If you want, you can add a soft felt sole inside the boot.

Beads

Materials: 2 skeins Lacy Løvegarn red # 15, about 830 translucent green 2.5-3 mm glass beads, liquid latex, 9 oz. (3.5 mm) sole leather, red leather dye, colorless edge finish.
Crochet hook: Size B1 (U.K. size 2)
Gauge: 14 sc x 15 rows using size B1 crochet hook = 2" X 2" (5 X 5 cm).
Size: This pattern is designed for a narrow size 8 ½ (European size 39), see page 92.

Altering the Size

You can alter the length of the foot by adding or subtracting 3 ch at the start for every ½" (1 cm) that your foot is longer or shorter than the size given.
Narrower foot: If you like, you can skip the 2nd and 13th round. If it is only the front of your foot that is narrower, you can skip the 6th round.
Wider foot: Repeat the 12th and 13th round, until the sole is wide enough. If you alter the slipper's size, remember to try it on frequently. You may need to also alter the part that fits over the top of the foot. This can be done by adding or subtracting sc in the upper's 3rd row.

Left sole

With a size B1 crochet hook, ch 64, sc around the entire foundation row.
Rnd 1: 62 sc, 3 sc in the next stitch. Put a red marking thread in the 2nd of the 3 stitches you have just cro-cheted. This is your first stitch (fs). Continue on the underside of the foundation row with: 61 sc, crochet 2 sc in the next st. Put a blue marking thread in the stitch you have just crocheted. This is your last stitch (ls).
Rnd 2: Work sc up to the fs, 3 sc in the fs. Work sc up to the ls, 3 sc in the ls.
Rnd 3: Repeat rnd 2. Drop yarn until the 5th rnd.
Rnd 4: This is a half round which is crocheted on the front part of the foot. Start in the 37th st from the ls, 24 sc, break the yarn. Skip 12 sts and start again, 30 sc, break the yarn.
Rnd 5: With yarn from rnd 3 repeat rnd 2. Drop yarn until the 7th rnd.
Rnd 6: This is a half round. Start in the 39th st from the ls, 20 sc, break the yarn. Skip 17 sts and start again, 30 sc, break the yarn.
In the following rounds sc as normal while increasing the in the indicated stitches.
Rnd 7: Heel: 1 inc. Toe: 3 sc in the fs. Heel: 1 inc, 1 sc, 1 sc in the ls.
Rnd 8: Heel: 4 sc, 1 inc. Toe: 3 sc in the fs. Heel: 1 inc, 4 sc, 1 sc in the ls. Drop yarn until the 11th round.
Rnd 9: This is a half round. With new yarn start in the 43rd st from the ls, 14 sc, break the yarn.
Rnd 10: This is a half round. With new yarn start in the 40th st from the ls, 20 sc, break the yarn.
Rnd 11: Pick up yarn from rnd 8. Heel: 1 sc, 1 inc. Toe: 3 sc in the fs.

Heel: 1 inc, 1 sc, 1 sc in the ls.
Rnd 12: Repeat rnd 8.
Rnd 13: Repeat rnd 11.
Rnd 14: Heel: 4 sc, 1 inc. Toe: 1 inc, 3 sc, 1 inc, 1 sl st, turn.
Now the upper can be crocheted.

Right sole
Crochet like the left sole except for the following rounds:
Rnd 4: Start in the 34th st from the ls, 30 sc, break the yarn. Skip 12 sts and start again, 24 sc, break the yarn.
Rnd 6: Start in the 36th st from the ls, 30 sc, break the yarn. Skip 17 sts and start again, 20 sc, break the yarn.

Rnd 9: Start in the 57th st before the ls, 14 sc, break the yarn.
Rnd 10: Start in the 60th st before the ls, 20 sc, break the yarn.

Note that this is a narrow design, so the widest point of your foot will be about ½" (1 cm) over the edges of the soles. Press the soles lightly with an iron so that they are flat. Lay them on a piece of paper and draw around them. These are the patterns you will use when you cut out your leather soles.

The Upper
Note that the upper is crocheted in sl st in order to connect this section of the slipper to the sole. These stitches should remain unworked.

Crocheting with Beads
There are many beads in this design. Don't try to put them all on the yarn at the same time. Break the yarn from time to time and put more beads on before continuing. Read more about working with beads on page 90.

The beads should be incorporated into every other single crochet stitch as follows: Work sc as usual.

When there are 2 loops on the crochet hook, push a bead in towards the work. Hook the yarn around the crochet hook, and pull it through the loops.
Rnd 1: Inc 1 sc in each of next 7 stitches = 14 sc, 2 sl st, turn.
Rnd 2: Crochet with beads, 2 sl st in the sole, turn.
Rnd 3: Sc, inc 1 sc in the first and last st, 2 sl st in the sole, turn.
Repeat the 2nd and 3rd round a total of 18 times. Follow with 1 round of crocheting with beads.

Edging and Assembly
Crochet beads into every sc on the edge.
Rnd 1: 20 sc, 15 ch, skip 10 st, 20 sc, 2 sl st in the sole, turn.
Rnd 2: Crochet with beads, 2 sl st in the sole, turn.
Rnd 3: 27 sc, 3 sc in the next stitch, 27 sc, 2 sl st in the sole, turn.
Rnd 4: Same as round 2, bind off.

Cut out 2 leather soles using your pattern. Coat the edges with red leather dye and colorless edge finish, as shown on page 91. Glue the soles on as shown on page 91.

Beads

Sunshine Boots

Materials: 4 skeins Lacy Løvegarn yellow # 20, about 720 clear yellow 2/5 to 3 mm glass beads, liquid latex.
Crochet Hook: Size B1 (U.K. size 2)
Gauge: 14 rows x 14 sc using size B1 crochet hook = 2" X 2" (5 X 5 cm).
Size: Girl's shoe size 8 ½-9 ½ (European size 26-27), see page 92.

Altering the Size

Altering the length: add or subtract 3 ch at the start for every ½" (1 cm) that your foot is longer or shorter than the size given.
Narrower foot: If you like, you can skip the 4th round. If it is only the front of your foot that is narrower, you can skip the 5th round.
Wider foot: Repeat the 1st round.
If you alter the boot's size, remember to try it on frequently. You may need to also alter the part that fits over the top of the foot. This part can be made wider by replace the 6th row with a repeat of the 4th row. If you want this part to be narrower, you can skip the increase in the 4th row.

But please note that if you make changes in the top of the foot and the leg on this design, you will have to change all the rows with loop stitches in order to get the loops placed correctly. You can also crochet fewer or more rows in the top surface and the leg of the boot in order to make it shorter or longer.

The Sole

With yellow yarn using and size B1 crochet hook ch 34, sc around the foundation row.
Rnd 1: 32 sc, 3 sc in the next stitch. Put a red marking thread in the 2nd of the 3 stitches you have just crocheted. This is your first stitch (fs). Continue on the otherside of the foundation row: 31 sc, crochet 2 sc in the next stitch. Put a blue marking thread in the stitch you have just crocheted. This is your last stitch (ls).
In the following rounds sc as normal while increasing the in the indicated stitches.
Rnd 2: Heel: 1 inc, 1 inc. Toe: 3 sc in the fs. Heel: 1 inc, 1 inc, 1 sc in the ls.
Rnd 3: Heel: 1 sc, 1 inc. Toe: 1 inc, 1 sc, 1 inc, 1 sc, 1 inc, 1 sc, 1 inc. Heel: 1 inc, 1 sc, 1 sc in the ls.
Rnd 4: Heel: 1 sc, 1 inc. Toe: 1 inc, 11 sc, 1 inc. Heel: 1 inc, 1 sc, 1 sc in the ls. Drop yarn until rnd 6.
Rnd 5: This is a half round, which is crocheted on the front part of the foot. Start in the 15th st from the ls. Toe: 3 sc in the center stitch. Finish in the 15th st before the ls.
Rnd 6: Pick up yarn from rnd 4. Heel: 3 sc, 1 inc. Toe: 1 inc, 1 sc, 1 inc, 1 sc, 1 inc, 1 sc, 1 inc. Heel: 1 inc, 3 sc, 1 sc in the ls. Drop yarn until rnd 8.
Rnd 7: This is a half round. Start in the 18th st from the ls. Toe: 1 inc, 21 sc, 1 inc. Finish in the 18th st before the ls.

Sunshine Boots

82

Rnd 8: Pick up yarn from rnd 8. Heel: 1 sc, 1 inc. Toe: 1 inc, 17 sc, 1 inc. Heel: 1 inc, 1 sc, 1 sc in the ls.

Rnd 9: Heel: 4 sc, 1 inc. Toe: 1 inc, 5 sc, 1 inc. Heel: 1 inc, 4 sc, 1 sc in the ls.

Rnd 10: Heel: 1 sc, 1 inc. Toe: 1 inc, 1 sc, 1 inc, 1 sc, 1 inc, 1 sc, 1 inc. Heel: 1 inc, 1 sc, 1 sc in the ls.

Rnd 11: Sc around.

Rnd 12: Work sc up to and including the fs. Crochet an additional 5 sc, 2 sl st, turn. Now you are ready to crochet the top of the slipper.

The Upper

Crochet lp st with 3 sc between the loops on the top of the slipper. Make the loops around a pencil, as explained on page 18.

Put 33 beads onto a separate skein of yarn, and switch to this skein while working the 1th row of the top of the slipper.

Note that the upper is crocheted in sl st in order to connect this section of the slipper to the sole. These stitches should remain unworked.

Row 1: 2 sc in each of the first 5 st, 3 sc in the fs, 2 sc in each of next 5 st = 23 sc. 2 sl st in the sole, turn.

Row 2: Sc, 2 sl st in the sole, turn.

Row 3: 3 sc, lp st, 2 sl st in the sole, turn.

Row 4: Sc, inc 1 sc in the first and last st, 2 sl st in the sole, turn.

Row 5, 6, 8, 9, 10, 12, 13, 14, 16, 17, 18, 20, 21, 22, 24, & 25: Sc, 2 sl st in the sole, turn.

Row 7, 15, & 23: 2 sc, lp st, 2 sl st in the sole, turn.

Row 11 & 19: 4 sc, lp st, 2 sl st in the sole, turn.

Row 26: Sc, (no sl st in the sole).

The Heel

The heel is worked back and forth along the heel section of the sole, and every row is attached to the upper with 2 sl st. Continue by using a loop from the upper. Remember, the sl st should always remain unworked.

Row 1-3: Sc, inc 2 sc evenly distributed throughout the row, 2 sc in the upper, turn.

Row 4: Sc, inc 2 sc evenly distributed throughout the round, break the yarn.

The Leg

The leg is crocheted into the stitches of the heel and upper. There are now 76 st in one row. If you have 1 st too few, you can crochet in the ls both at the beginning and end of the 1st row. Put 171 beads onto the yarn. Start at the ls.

Row 1: Sc across, turn with 1 ch.

Row 2: 1 sc, lp st, turn with 1 ch.

Row 3: Sc across, turn with 1 ch.

Row 4: Sc across, turn with 1 ch.

Row 5: Sc across, turn with 1 ch.

Row 6: 3 sc, lp st, turn with 1 ch.

Row 7: Sc across, turn with 1 ch.

Row 8: Sc across, turn with 1 ch.

Crochet the above 8 rows a total of 8 times, and repeat the 1-4 row one additional time = 68 rows. Switch crochet hooks, and put the rest of the beads onto the yarn once the first 171 beads have been used.

Assembly

Use a scrap of yarn to sew the leg of the boot together up the back through the outermost loops. Make sure that the rows line up evenly. Put liquid latex on the soles as shown on page 90.

Winter-blue Slippers with Ice Crystals

Winter-blue Slippers with Ice Crystals

Materials: 2 skeins Lacy Løveg-arn ice blue # 62, 3 mm glass beads (about 420 clear, about 80 clear light blue), liquid latex, 9 oz. (3.5 mm) sole leather.

Crochet Hook: Size B1 (U.K. size 2)

Gauge: 14 sc x 15 rows using size B1 crochet hook = 2" X 2" (5 X 5 cm)

Size: Shoe size 7 ½ (European size 38), see page 92.

Altering the Size

Altering the length of the foot: add or subtract 3 ch at the start for every ½" (1 cm) that your foot is longer or shorter than the size given.

Narrower foot. If you like, you can skip the 13th and 14th round.

Wider foot: Repeat the 12th, 13th & 14th round, until the sole is wide enough. If your foot is very wide, it may be necessary to increase 4 single crochet stitches in a couple of the rounds instead of 2 as suggested. This will be indicated by the work in progress buckling noticeably along the edges.

When you alter the slipper's size, you should try it on frequently. You may need to also alter the part that fits over the top of the foot (15-43 round). Instead of the 2 sc increase in every other row, you might want to just add 1 inc in some rows. In any case, take the increase in the center-most stitches of the rows. You can of course also add increases on the sides and in the middle of a row if you need to.

The Sole

With size B1 crochet hook ch 50, sc around the foundation row.

Rnd 1: 48 sc, 3 sc in the next st. Put a red marking thread in the 2nd of the 3 stitches you have just crocheted. This is your first stitch (fs). Continue on the underside of the foundation row: 47 sc, crochet 2 sc in the next stitch. Put a blue marking thread in the stitch you have just crocheted. This is your last stitch (ls).

Rnd 2: Work sc up to your fs, 3 sc in the fs. Work sc up to your ls, 3 sc in the ls.

In the following rounds sc as normal while increasing the in the indicated stitches.

Rnd 3: Heel: 1 inc, 1 inc. Toe: 3 sc in the fs. Heel: 1 inc, 1 inc, 1 sc, 1 sc in the ls.

Rnd 4: Heel: 1 sc, 1 inc. Toe: 1 inc, 1

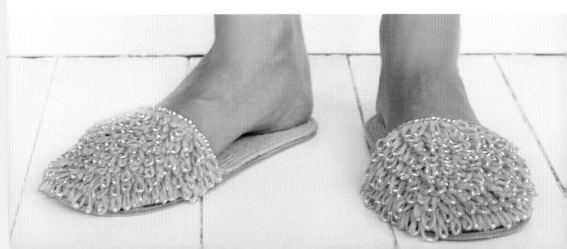

sc, 1 inc, 1 sc, 1 inc, 1 sc, 1 inc. Heel: 1 inc, 1 sc, 1 sc in the ls.

Rnd 5: Heel: 4 sc, 1 inc. Toe: 1 inc, 5 sc, 1 inc. Heel: 1 inc, 4 sc, 1 sc in the ls.

Rnd 6: Heel: 1 sc, 1 inc. Toe: 1 inc, 11 sc, 1 inc. Heel: 1 inc, 1 sc, 1 sc in the ls. Drop yarn until rnd 8.

Rnd 7: This is a half round, which is crocheted on the front part of the foot. Start in the 28th st from the ls. Toe: 3 sc in the fs. End in the 28th st before the ls.

Rnd 8: Pick up yarn from rnd 6. Heel: 3 sc, 1 inc. Toe: 1 inc, 1 sc, 1 inc, 1 sc, 1 inc, 1 sc, 1 inc. Heel: 1 inc, 3 sc, 1 sc in the ls. Drop yarn until rnd 10.

Rnd 9: This is a half round. Start in the 32nd st from the ls. Toe: 1 inc, 21 sc, 1 inc. End in the 32nd st before the ls.

Rnd 10: Pick up yarn from rnd 8. Heel: 1 sc, 1 inc. Toe: 1 inc, 17 sc, 1 inc. Heel: 1 inc, 1 sc, 1 sc in the ls. Drop yarn until rnd 12.

Rnd 11: This is a half round. Start in the 36th st from the ls. Toe: 1 inc, 23 sc, 1 inc. End in the 36th st before the ls.

Rnd 12: Pick up yarn from rnd 10. Heel: 2 sc, 1 inc. Toe: 1 inc, 19 sc, 1 inc. Heel: 1 inc, 2 sc, 1 sc in the ls.

Rnd 13: Heel: 4 sc, 1 inc. Toe: 1 inc, 13 sc, 1 inc. Heel: 1 inc, 4 sc, 1 sc in the ls.

Rnd 14: Toe: 1 inc, 9 sc, 1 inc. Continue crocheting 3 sc and 2 sl st, turn. Now you are ready to work the top of the slipper.

Press the soles lightly with an iron so that they are flat. Lay them on a piece of paper and draw around them. These are the patterns you will use when you cut out your leather soles.

The Upper

Note that the upper is crocheted in sl st in order to connect this section of the slipper to the sole. These stitches should remain unworked.

Break the yarn, wax the end of the yarn, and draw about 210 clear beads onto the yarn as shown on page 90. Continue after the 14th round as follows:

Row 1: 19 sc, 2 sl st in the sole, turn.

Row 2 and all even rows: Lp st around a pen or pencil that measures about .05" (1.5 mm) in circumference, with 1 sc between the loops, as shown on page 18. Attach 1 bead in every loop, 2 sl st in the sole, turn.

Row 3 and all odd rows until the 19th row: Inc 1 sc in the first and last st, 2 sl st in the sole, turn.

Row 21 and all odd rows until the 27th row: Sc, 2 sl st in the sole, turn.

Row 29: Sc, 1 sl st in the sole, cut the yarn and weave the ends in.

Assembly

Sew the light-blue beads along the edge of the slippers. Cut out two leather soles using the paper pattern you made earlier, and glue them on using liquid latex, as described on page 91.

Happy Stripes

Materials: 1 skein Cosy Wool Løveg-arn in each of the following colors: light blue # 66, raw white # 30, red # 17, petroleum # 68, pink # 12, green # 71, liquid latex, 9 oz. (3.5 mm) sole leather, blue leather dye, colorless edge finish.

Crochet Hook: Size E4 (U.K. size 3½)

Gauge: 10 sc x 11 rows using size E4 crochet hook = 2" X 2" (5 X 5 cm).

Altering the Size

Size: This design, which is spacious across the front of the foot, is intended for shoe size 7 ½ (European size 38) see page 92.

Altering the length: For every ½" (1 cm) that your foot is longer or short er than the pattern, add or subtract 4 ch at the start. This means that the number of stitches you will crochet before, during and after the increases will be changed by 1, 2, and 1.

For example: If you want the slipper to be ½" (1 cm) longer, create a chain of 191 + 4 = 195 ch + 1 sl st, and in the second round change to: 1 ch, 47 sc, 1 inc, 2 sc, 1 inc, 94 sc, 1 inc, 2 sc, 1 inc, 47 sc, and end with 1 sl in a ch.

If you want to alter the width of the section, you can add or subtract 1 round of sc. The width will be altered by ½" (1 cm) (and the slipper's circumference by 3/4" (2 cm)) every time you change the pattern by 1 round.

Crochet 191 ch in turquoise yarn,

make a circle with 1 sl st at the same time as you switch to the light blue yarn = 192 ch total

Rnd 1 (with light blue): 1 ch, sc, end with 1 sl st in ch.

Rnd 2: 1 ch, 46 sc, 1 inc, 2 sc, 1 inc, 92 sc, 1 inc, 2 sc, 1 inc, 46 sc, end with 1 sl st in ch.

Rnd 3 (with white): 1 ch, 47 sc, 1 inc, 2 sc, 1 inc, 94 sc, 1 inc, 2 sc, 1 inc, 47 sc, end with 1 sl st in ch.

Rnd 4 (with green): 1 ch, 48 sc, 1 inc, 2 sc, 1 inc, 96 sc, 1 inc, 2 sc, 1 inc, 48 sc, end with 1 sl st in ch.

Rnd 5: 1 ch, 49 sc, 1 inc, 2 sc, 1 inc, 98 sc, 1 inc, 2 sc, 1 inc, 49 sc, end with 1 sl st in ch.

Rnd 6 (with white): 1 ch, 50 sc, 1 inc, 2 sc, 1 inc, 100 sc, 1 inc, 2 sc, 1 inc, 50 sc, end with 1 sl st in ch.

Rnd 7 (with light blue): 1 ch, sc, end with 1 sl st in ch.

Rnd 8 (with red): 1 ch, sc, end with 1 sl st in ch.

Rnd 9 (with white): 1 ch, sc, end with 1 sl st in ch.

Rnd 10 (with pink): 1 ch, sc, end with 1 sl st in ch.

Rnd 11 (with turquoise): 1 ch, sc, end with 1 sl st in ch, break the yarn.

Crochet the inside of the ring (the turquoise ch row you began with) together with sl st. Remember to crochet on the wrong side of the work. You should crochet from increase to increase with the turquoise yarn. Put the crochet hook through one loop from each side so that the parts where it is crocheted together doesn't become too thick.

Fold the work together, and crochet the slipper's bottom together using slip stitches with turquoise yarn. Crochet the round part of the toes forward until the toes are covered.

Ankle strap
Begin with the ls.
Row 1 (with red): 1 ch, crochet 27 sc, skip the corresponding st in the other half of the slipper, crochet 27 sc, end with 1 sl st in ch.
Row 2 (with red): Same as row 1.
Row 3 (with green): Same as row 1.
Weave in the ends.

Happy Stripes

The Soles
Cut out the soles using the pattern on page 92. The soles are quite wide and long, so you will be able to see their edges if you look down at your foot from above. If you have changed the size of the pattern, you will need to draw your own sole pattern, and should make it extend .075" (2 mm) from the edge of the design.

When you have roughened the surface of the soles, apply the blue leather dye and colorless edge finish all the way out on the soles and on the edges. Glue the soles on using liquid latex, as shown on page 91.

Stitches, tips and techniques

Pompons

Satin Stitch

Running Stitches

Chain Stitch

Running Stitches with Overcasting

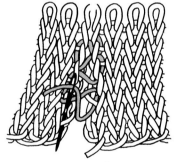

Mattress Stitch

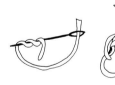

French Knots

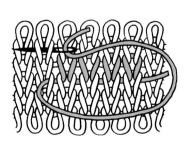

Kitchener's Stitch

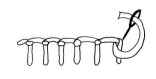

Button Hole Stitch

Beads

Many of the designs in this book are decorated with beads. Traditional glass beads look very attractive and can be used with all kinds of techniques.

When buying beads, it is important to select ones that have a large enough hole that the waxed end of a piece of yarn can be pulled through it. If you follow the bead sizes that I recommend in the instructions, the holes in the beads should be appropriate for the yarn being used. If you want to be certain, take a waxed piece of yarn with you and try a bead before buying.

Use a piece of beeswax to wax the end of the yarn before putting it through a bead. Pull about 2.5" to 2.75" (6 to 7 cm) of the yarn through the beeswax so that the end becomes narrow and firm. Roll the end of the yarn in your hand, and between your fingers, to get the beeswax worked into the yarn. Cut the end of the yarn at a bit of an angle, and use the yarn end as a needle.

Push the beads further in on the piece of yarn as you put add more beads. Leave them there, and pick up beads from there as you need them.

In the designs that call for a large number of beads, you can start by putting just a few on the yarn in the beginning. You can then break the yarn and put more beads on it as the work progresses.

Rubber Soles

Rubber soles make your slippers both more durable and less slippery. They also allow the foot its greatest freedom of movement.

Materials: Liquid latex.

Tools: Blackboard chalk, clothes pins, scrap of foam rubber, and talcum powder or similar powder.

Place the slipper on a board. Use a sharp piece of chalk to draw a thin line on the board around the outline of the slipper. When you have sketched out the area, brush liquid latex over the shape. Grab hold of the small piece of foam rubber with the clothes pin. Dip the foam rubber into the liquid latex, and press it onto the sole of the slipper.

When the liquid latex has turned clear yellow, the sole is dry and you can continue working on the slipper. Give each slipper 3 to 4 layers. Sprinkle a little talcum powder over the sole before you use it so that it isn't sticky when you walk. This treatment can be repeated if the soles every wear out.

Leather Soles

Leather soles are both attractive and durable. They make the slippers sturdier so they don't slide around on the foot.

Materials: Liquid latex, 9 oz. (3.5 mm) sole leather.

Tools: Sharp hobby knife, glass cutter, blackboard chalk, clothes pins, scrap of foam rubber, and a coarse file, brush or very coarse sandpaper for roughing up the surface.

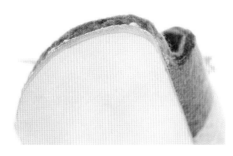

Draw the shape of the slippers on the sole leather using a ball point pen, and cut them out using a sharp hobby knife. If your edges are uneven you can even them out using the sharp edge of a class cutter. Rasp the side of the soles that will be glued onto the slippers using a coarse file, a brush, or very coarse sandpaper. Be very thorough. Remove any dust. Put a layer of liquid latex on the soles, and give the slippers two layers, or as many as you need to in order to create a smooth surface of latex without any little yarn fibers sticking through. Allow all the parts to dry overnight.

Check to make sure that the liquid latex forms a smooth surface. If there are areas that are not quite covered with liquid latex, add another layer and let it dry again overnight. When the liquid latex covers the entire surface and is completely dry, glue the soles onto the slippers, pressing them firmly in place.

Leather Dye and Colorless Edge Finish

In this book leather dye is used to color the edges of all the leather soles. You can apply the dye with the brush that comes with it or with a swab stick if the brush is too big. If you want a darker shade on the edges of the soles, just apply a second coat of the leather dye. When the soles have achieved the shade you desire, put on a layer of colorless edge finish using a swab stick. This will help keep the dye from rubbing off.

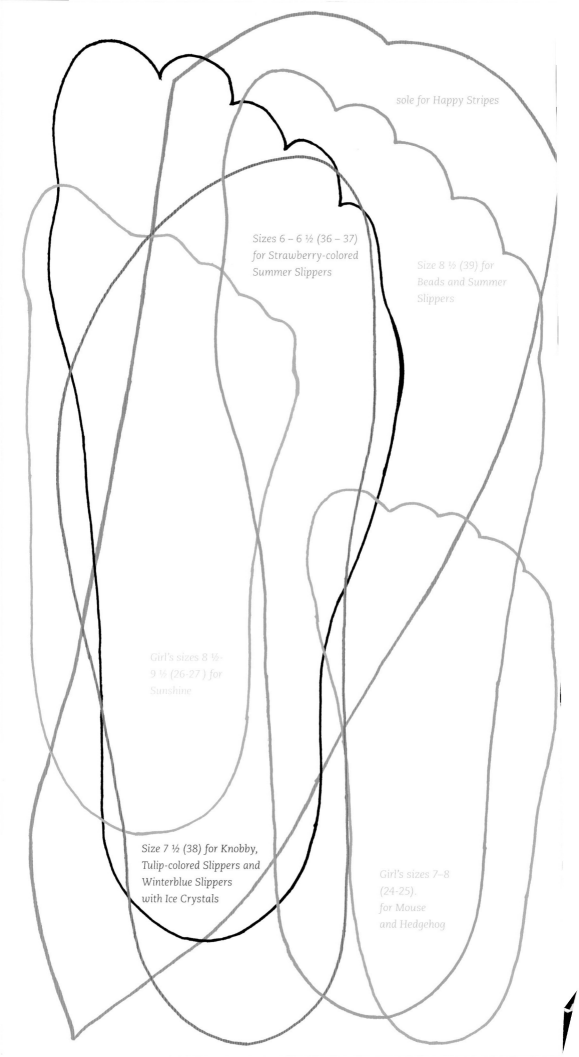

sole for Happy Stripes

Sizes 6 – 6 ½ (36 – 37) for Strawberry-colored Summer Slippers

Size 8 ½ (39) for Beads and Summer Slippers

Girl's sizes 8 ½-9 ½ (26-27) for Sunshine

Size 7 ½ (38) for Knobby, Tulip-colored Slippers and Winterblue Slippers with Ice Crystals

Girl's sizes 7–8 (24-25). for Mouse and Hedgehog

Templates and sizes: Use these templates to check your foot's size against that which is given in the pattern instructions.

. . . .

Suppliers List

Halcyon Yarn
12 School Street
Bath, ME 04530
800-341-0282
www.halcyonyarn.com
service@halcyonyarn.com

Webs—America's Yarn Store
75 Service Center Road
Northampton, MA 01060
800-367-9327
www.yarn.com
customerservice@yarn.com

Westminster Fibers Inc.
165 Ledge Street
Nashua, NH 03060
800-445-9276
www.westminsterfibers.com
rowan@westminsterfibers.com

For help choosing a suitable yarn substitution contact one of the suppliers above.

Helpful information for yarn substitutions:

Fonty Kidopale: (compares to Rowan Kid silk haze) 70% kid mohair/30% polyamide, 25 gr = 250 meters

HP Løve Baby and Hose Yarn: (baby and sock yarn) 80% wool/20 % poly-amide, 50 g = 210 m

Roma Løvegarn: (it is a metallic yarn, not completely even) 80% viscose/20% metallic polyester, 25 g = 325 m

Fonty Angora: 30% angora/70% merino wool, 25 g = 125 m

Nuuk Løvegarn: 50% wool/15% alpaca/35% acrylic, 100 g = 60 m

Cosy Wool Løvegarn: 100% wool, 100 g = 125 m

Hjerte Blend: a blend of cotton and synthetic 50/50, 50 g = ca. 150 m

Highland Løvegarn: 40% wool/60% acrylic, 50 g – 85 m

Cotmondo Cotton: 100% cotton, 50 g = 80 m

Heavy Løvegarn: 60% cotton/40%, 50 g = 65 m

Lacy Løvegarn: 50% cotton/50% acrylic, 50 g = 125 m

Corriedale Wool
Hose Yarn (sock yarn)
Rustico Lovegarn